D0930552

Cultural Studies of Delaware and the Eastern Shore
An Occasional Series Published by the University of Delaware Press

2001
Jones, Jacqueline. *Creek Walking: Growing Up in Delaware in the 1950s.*

2000
Boyer, William. *Governing Delaware: Policy Problems in the First State.*
Hoffecker, Carol E. *Honest John Williams: U.S. Senator, 1947–1970.*
Pifer, Drury. *Hanging the Moon: The Rollins Rise to Riches.*
Scott, Jane Harrington. *Caesar Rodney: A Gentleman and a Whig.*
Shores, David. *Tangier Island: People, Place, and Talk.*

1999
Young, Toni. *Becoming American; Remaining Jewish: The Story of Wilmington, Delaware's First Jewish Community, 1879–1924.*

1995
Hoffecker, Carol E., Richard Waldron, Lorraine E. Williams, and Barbara E. Benson, eds. *New Sweden in America.*

1993
Munroe, John A. *History of Delaware* (3rd edition).

1990
Schlenther, Boyd Stanley. *Charles Thomson: A Patriot's Pursuit.*

1989
Custer, Jay F. *Prehistoric Cultures of the Delmarva Peninsula: An Archaeological Study.*
Sweeney, John A. *Grandeur on the Appoquinimink: The House of William Corbit at Odessa, Delaware.*

1988
Bushman, Claudia L., Harold B. Hancock, and Elizabeth Moyne Homsey, eds. *Minutes of the House of Assembly of the Delaware State, 1781–1792.*

1986
Bushman, Claudia L., Harold B. Hancock, and Elizabeth Moyne Homsey, eds. *Proceedings of the Assembly of the Lower Counties on Delaware 1770–1776, of the Constitutional Convention of 1776, and of the House of Assembly of the Delaware State 1776–1781.*
Custer, Jay F., ed. *Late Woodland Cultures of the Middle Atlantic Region.*

1984
Custer, Jay F. *Delaware Prehistoric Archaeology: An Ecological Approach*
Munroe, John A. *History of Delaware* (2nd edition).

1983
Weslager, C. A. *The Nanticoke Indians—Past and Present.*

1979
Munroe, John A. *History of Delaware* (1st edition).

1977
Hancock, Harold. *The Loyalties of Revolutionary Delaware.*

1973
Hoffecker, Carol E., ed., *Readings in Delaware History.*

CREEK WALKING
Growing Up in Delaware
in the 1950s

Jacqueline Jones

DELAWARE

Newark: University of Delaware Press
London: Associated University Presses

© 2001 by Jacqueline Jones

Associated University Presses
440 Forsgate Drive
Cranbury, NJ 08512

Associated University Presses
16 Barter Street
London WC1A 2AH, England

Associated University Presses
P.O. Box 338, Port Credit
Mississauga, Ontario
Canada L5G 4L8

The paper used in this publication meets the requirements of the American National Standard for Permanence of Paper for Printed Library Materials Z39.48–1984.

Library of Congress Cataloging-in-Publication Data

Jones, Jacqueline, 1948–
    Creek walking : growing up in Delaware in the 1950s / Jacqueline Jones.
        p. cm. — (Cultural studies of Delaware and the Eastern Shore)
    Includes index.
    ISBN 0-87413-754-3 (alk. paper)
    1. Jones, Jacqueline, 1948—Childhood and youth. 2. Christiana (Del.)—
Biography. 3. Christiana (Del.)—Social life and customs—20th century. 4. City and town life—Delaware—Christiana. 5. Girls—Delaware—Christiana—
Biography. I. Title. II. Series.

F174.C57 J66 2001
975.1′1—dc21

                                                                    2001027252

PRINTED IN THE UNITED STATES OF AMERICA

This book is dedicated to the children of the
Albert H. Jones Elementary School in Christiana, Delaware,
and to the memory of my father

Contents

Acknowledgments

In the mid-twentieth century, the town of Christiana, Delaware, was an unprepossessing-looking place, and fifty years later the tiny crossroads had almost disappeared from view, lost in a maze of super-highways, shopping malls, and office parks. And so I am grateful to the many individuals who shared with me the conviction that the story of Christiana was worthy of a larger audience. My greatest debt is to my mother, Sylvia Phelps Jones, who offered crucial support at all stages of the project. She kept a newspaper-clipping file, dug deep into her own memory for information about our extended family, located books and articles on Delaware history, checked names and dates, and corrected me whenever my memory failed me (as she put it). I benefited from her considerable knowledge of the history of Delaware in general and the history of Christiana in particular. Her love and generosity played a large part in the writing of this book.

My brothers, Kent and Randy Jones, and my cousin Southard Jones good-naturedly reminisced about our childhood together, and all three read and commented upon a completed draft of the manuscript. Pat Jones, Barbara Jones, and Tonya Price offered their expert opinions on the folkways of the Jones and Phelps families.

I also relied upon Patricia Johnson Paparelli, Thelma Johnson, and Ella Rineer for their perspectives on Christiana in the 1950s. At the Albert H. Jones Elementary School in Christiana, Rick Bartkowski, the principal; Vicki Carew, the vice-principal; and Donna Lyle, a fourth-grade teacher, helped to make our visit to the school in January, 1999, a memorable experience for my mother and me. I am especially grateful to the friendly, high-spirited children in Ms. Lyle's fourth-grade class, who took time out from their studies to answer my questions about their families and school.

Mildred Smith of Christiana graciously granted me permission to use her painting of the Shannon Inn, and Eric Crossan took the photo of it. The Camera Place in Wellesley, Massachusetts, did a beautiful job of reproducing and preparing a number of old family photographs for publication.

At the University of Delaware Press, Carol E. Hoffecker took an interest in the project at its earliest stages. Editor Donald C. Mell pointed the way toward revisions. My copyeditor, Karen Druliner, provided me with many helpful suggestions, ranging from the substantive to the stylistic. Rita McWhorter prepared the index, and Anne Krulikowski went to a great deal of time and trouble to locate the maps. At Associated University Presses, Julien Yoseloff and Christine Retz guided the manuscript through the production process.

At Brandeis University, Judy Brown and Dona Delorenzo used their technological wizardry to help me negotiate different computer disks and word processing packages.

Other friends, family members, and acquaintances encouraged me to persist in transforming a collection of memories into a book. Al and Rose Abramson and Karin Lifter offered heartfelt support. Sigrid Bergenstein invited me to speak about the project before the Sisterhood of Temple Beth Elohim in Wellesley, and that audience gave me a warm and enthusiastic reception for which I am most grateful.

For many years my daughters, Sarah and Anna Abramson, and my husband, Jeffrey Abramson, have listened to me tell Christiana stories in bits and pieces. Suburbanites all, they have maintained a level of fascination and skepticism that I found positively inspiring. I thank them for their love, and for listening.

CREEK WALKING

Introduction

This book is about a small town and the people who lived there in the 1950s, as seen through the eyes of a little girl then and as interpreted by a social historian now, forty years later. In the following pages, several overlapping stories unfold—the story of a Mid-Atlantic trading post transformed over the course of three centuries; the story of a tiny, virtually all-Protestant community nevertheless crisscrossed by a variety of social groupings; and the story of a child wedged between two extended families, strikingly divergent in style. Like all lives, mine consisted of layers, compressed but still distinct. My temperament was shaped by a peculiar family culture, which was in turn enmeshed in the institutions of church and school revealing of a particular time and place—the first twelve years of my life, from 1948 to 1960, in Christiana, Delaware.

Christiana was and is a commercial crossroads, albeit one that has changed dramatically over the generations, producing sets of winners and losers at each stage of development. In the seventeenth century, the Leni-Lenape Indians, situated between two major rivers, the Delaware and the Susquehanna, in what is now north-central Delaware, began to abandon their subsistence way of life in favor of trading beaver pelts with European colonists. This switch—from hunting and fishing for food, to hunting for commercial exchange—eventually contributed to the dispersion and demise of the group. Subsequently, in the eighteenth century, a village called Christiana Bridge grew along the banks of the Christina River, a waterway connecting the Delaware River to the Maryland hinterland and beyond. By the 1790s Christiana Bridge was a bustling entrepôt, its wharves piled high with barrels of flour milled in New Jersey and Pennsylvania and bound for the backcountry. Within a generation, however, canals, turnpikes, and railroads had bypassed the town, causing it to fall into a stupor from which it was not aroused until the latter part of the

13

twentieth century. At that point it was the town's proximity to an interstate highway, I-95, that fueled its economic revival.

Christiana's latest incarnation is a place called Metroform, an expanse of health-care services, schools, hotels, restaurants and retail stores, all connected by traffic-choked highways and anchored by a huge shopping mall. The mall draws customers from New Jersey, Pennsylvania, and Maryland as well as the surrounding New Castle County. In effect, on the site of the old residential Christiana a new retail community has arisen, one marked not by a small knot of people who think of themselves as neighbors, but by random encounters of consumers who come for part of a day, spend some money, and then return to their homes. The natural landscape as I knew it has been largely obliterated by this new crossroads. Moreover, Christiana has become embedded in a national economy, now that the county's local financial services industry provides employment and a middle-class way of life for thousands of people who migrate into the area each year. Over the generations, then, the scattered bands of Leni-Lenape have yielded to the residents of the compact little port village on the banks of the Christina, which today has metamorphosed into a textbook case of suburban sprawl. Yet one could argue that Christiana retains its original character as a place that is testament to the American commercial impulse, whether that impulse manifests itself in the distribution of beaver skins, barrels of grain, credit cards, or Big Macs.

In the 1950s, social diversity Christiana-style took the form of theological and ritualistic cleavages between the Presbyterians and the Methodists. Indeed, viewed from afar, in its relative homogeneity the town seemed to represent a Norman Rockwellian (or George Orwellian, depending on one's point of view) vision of American life. Consisting of no more than 400 or so souls, about 320 of them with white skins and 80 with black, with a preponderance of rural and working-class folk, Christiana was home to an inward-looking, even insular, lot. Still, almost all of the wage earners worked somewhere else. And so ours was a split vision; the town afforded a place to gossip, worship and go to school, but provided almost no opportunities to make or spend money.

A closer look reveals a population that, while small, was richly variegated in social terms—blacks and whites; natives and recent in-migrants; old-timers and youngsters; men and women; young and old; and groups defined by religion, by place of origin (Appalachia or New England for example), and by the color of their work-collars (blue, white, or pink). My immediate family offered a shining example of post-World War II middle-class prosperity. Though we did not live in the suburbs, we possessed the material trappings of a newly affluent society. And yet just as significant, and more intriguing in my view, was the way my parents straddled two riotously different family cultures, with straitlaced Phelpses on one side and freewheeling Joneses on the other. All this is to say that, for a curious child, even the village of Christiana offered a rich experimental lab for observing human nature and social organization.

The themes explored here range from, at one extreme, my own efforts to sort out what I owed myself and what I owed other people, to, at the other extreme, historic developments that have shaped the Mid-Atlantic states through the centuries. In its brashness this enterprise would seem to mandate multiple forms of storytelling, including elements of memoir, local history, family genealogy, cultural anthropology, and social and economic history. My original intention was to blend these forms seamlessly, reflecting the way we live our lives.

So I was somewhat surprised to discover that the pieces of my childhood did not always fit together with pieces of history, or at least not as snugly as I had hoped. Where I sought a mosaic I more often found fragments. As a collection of people we were ignorant about our past, oblivious to the role of Christiana in a series of dynamic Delaware Valley economies, and indifferent toward the region's racist past. Whites distanced themselves from their black neighbors, and segregated schools and churches enforced historic injustices toward black people as a group. Even within the relatively circumscribed realm of evangelical Protestantism, denominational loyalties divided congregants. Though broadly similar in terms of church liturgy and discipline, the white Presbyterians and the white and black Methodists remained largely estranged from one another. Nor did family ties necessarily produce family feeling. The two sides of my own family— my father's mother and brother on one side, and my mother's parents and siblings on the other—all lived in close proximity, but they did not overlap at work, in school, in church, or even, for the most part, during secular or religious celebrations or holidays. Thus my parents and brothers and I contended, at times uneasily, with two divergent sets of kin-based folkways.

For my part, I early embraced the stance of observer, the town to my eyes so full of drama and intrigue, albeit on a modest scale. Every day I lived out the labels assigned to me as a Presbyterian white girl raised in a middle-class family. As I became aware of those labels, I began to detach myself from them. This detachment was perhaps the root of who and what I eventually became—a Jew, a scholar, and a New Englander.

The writer Frank McCourt maintains that "the happy childhood is hardly worth your while." I beg to disagree. It is true that some would claim that I labor under the curse of the memoirist—I am heir to a happy childhood—because the following pages contain no first-hand accounts of trauma or abuse, of fabulous wealth or grinding poverty. However, in its relative uneventfulness my own childhood is no doubt evocative of many others, and in its outlines—the daily tasks of going to school, negotiating family relationships and growing up, all within a culture of security and material comfort—at least suggestive of the broader forces shaping American life in the mid-twentieth century.

This book is both less and more than a conventional memoir—less because it is so limited time-wise, a mere dozen years at mid-century, and a snapshot of the town four decades after that; but more because it is part of a larger historical inquiry flowing from my area of scholarly research. Growing up in Christiana prompted my interest in African American history. White residents of the town, my own family included, accepted as "natural" the second-class status of blacks, as that status had evolved through generations of legalized discrimination and prejudice. Yet by the mid-1950s it was clear that blacks in Delaware, and throughout the country, were challenging history and its verities. The famous 1954 Supreme Court decision *Brown vs. the Board of Education* led to the integration of Christiana Elementary School in the fall of 1956. That year, the appearance of a single African American girl in my third-grade class alerted me to the possibility that what had occurred in the past (in this case, the triumph of state-sanctioned prejudice) need not prevail in the future. History mattered, but it did not consist of a collection of foreordained (or, in a term used by our Presbyterian minister, predestined) events. To affirm the claims of Christiana's black citizens, then, was to call into question the strictures of family, and the meaning of faith itself. History was a story of transformation, not a blueprint for life in the present.

I would spend my adult life exploring historical contingencies, the myriad forces that shaped specific American places at any particular time. From an initial focus on African American history, my work broadened to studies of regional economic change, and the impact of that change on patterns of work—what groups of people labored at which jobs, how, why, and under what conditions. When I revisited Christiana at the end of the twentieth century, now as a history professor, I learned for the first time of the town's successive economies over a period of four hundred years. Growing up in the mid-twentieth century, I had inhabited a time far removed from the heyday of the port in the 1790s, and more than a generation before the retail and service boom of the 1980s. Only recently have I learned that the town's history consists not of a linear-smooth chronology, but rather of a series of stories marked by fits and starts.

In telling these stories I have tried to avoid the two models commonly employed by historians in describing change over time. One narrative, the declension view of history, would encourage us to mourn the passing of small-town America and the pollution of the pond in my parents' backyard, to lament the encroaching tangle of interstate highways in northern Delaware, even as I might mourn and lament the loss of my own childhood. The elementary school I attended still exists, but its pupils come from Wilmington and other far reaches of New Castle County, and hardly anyone walks home any more. Indeed, as a readily identifiable place—as a physical space and as the site of a shared consciousness among the people who live there—the town of Christiana no longer exists.

In contrast, proponents of the Whiggish view of history would stress progress and growth through the years. In this view, Christiana has at last overcome its sad past of the last century and a half, and has emerged into the twenty-first century as a small but emblematic cog in the global economy. The town is, moreover, a much more lively and racially integrated place than it was forty years ago. In a parallel vein, I grew up, attended graduate school, and decided to work and raise a family in another place—a classic American story of migration and social mobility. In my own life, I have much more to celebrate than to mourn.

Alas, neither of these narratives captures the complexity of the town's stories, its history. Christiana was never much of a cohesive community when I was growing up there, if by that we mean a group of people bound by what they have in common with one another. I shall leave it to the reader to judge the validity of a pronouncement I make to my students: The only people who romanticize life in a small town (and there are many, at least among scholars today) are the people who have never lived in one. I am only half joking.

In order to protect the privacy of non-family members, I have used pseudonyms in referring to Christiana residents of the 1950s.

My father, Albert H. Jones, began a long and distinguished career in public service as a member of the Christiana school board in 1956. He believed in the redemptive power of public education, the ideal of kids from all different backgrounds learning together in the same classroom. Today the school in Christiana named in his honor struggles to uphold that ideal, but pervasive residential segregation by income and by race continues to separate people into different neighborhoods even as their children come together everyday at school. This book is dedicated to my father's memory, to the children of Christiana, and to the still unfulfilled promise of American public education.

1

Delaware Buffalo

My aunts all looked alike—short and bespectacled, their pin-straight brown hair softly permanent-waved. On Sunday mornings they congregated arrayed in rayon floral-print dresses, short white gloves, and discreet little hats, Presbyterian Church Ladies all. Or so it seemed to outsiders. Whenever one of my older cousins would introduce her new boyfriend to us, a ritual reserved for the annual Fourth of July picnic, the apparent fungibility of my aunts became clear to me; newcomers to the family circle found it hard to tell them apart and keep their names straight.

Counting my mother, the Phelps-family aunts numbered eight, seven of them daughters of an unlikely matriarch, the grandmother I saw virtually every day of the first twelve years of my life, until her death in 1961. By the time I came along she was bent over from the crippling effects of osteoporosis, a condition no doubt exacerbated by the fact that she had borne eight children over a fifteen-year period, from 1904 (the year her oldest, an only son, was born), and in 1905, 1906, 1909, 1911, 1912, and 1915, until 1919 (the year my mother, the youngest, was born). My grandmother wore her hair, still jet black with only a trace of gray, in a single, waist-long braid wrapped on top of her head. Both she and her husband my grandfather believed bobbed hair to be an unwelcome departure from good old-fashioned womanly decorum.

When I tell about the aunts I must make it clear that I have a particular subset in mind—the four sisters who, along with my mother, lived within an eight-mile radius of the Phelps homestead in Christiana, a small town in central New Castle County, Delaware. Together, my aunts, uncles and cousins provided a kind of emotional ballast for my childhood. Their Sunday afternoon visits to my grandmother's house, which was next door to our own, constituted the highlight of my week when I was growing up, and the focal point of my memories later in life. My only Phelps uncle had a Phelps-like

19

wife; she was similar to his sisters in temperament and values, and upon marriage, she became a member of the family not only in name but in spirit. The two oldest sisters, together with their husbands, had moved out of the area—one to Oklahoma and one to Missouri—returning to Delaware only sporadically.

I had another aunt, a non-Phelps, or more accurately, an anti-Phelps, a Jones by marriage. The Joneses, consisting of my father's brother and his wife and their four sons, lived only a couple of miles from us in the village of Ogletown, but remained far removed from the sedate and predictable world of my mother's family. Drinkers and takers-of-the-Lord's-name-in-vain, my Jones aunt and uncle maintained an eclectic household that consisted of not only my four cousins (all boys and all prone to what we called "roughhousing"), but also a bizarre assortment of animals, wild and domesticated. On Sunday afternoon, while the Phelpses were discreetly amusing themselves with talk about church politics, the Joneses were more likely to be mixing cocktails and highballs, and regaling guests with stories about their high-spirited horses and loyal bird dogs. My uncle punctuated these tales with his explosive laughter.

Though my grandparents arrived in 1924 and were relative newcomers to the town of Christiana, the Phelpses had early assumed the mantle of the local landed gentry. In contrast, the nearby city of Wilmington was the province of the Joneses, for that is where this generation of the clan originated, and that is where my father worked and his mother lived, and had always lived. Just ten miles away from Christiana, a half hour drive up Route 13, Wilmington was a vibrant city of 100,000, and as far as we were concerned, it had all the cosmopolitan features of Manhattan. Headquarters of the DuPont and Hercules chemical companies, the city boasted a few conspicuously large office buildings, a world-class hotel, and, in the surrounding area, a variety of museums, hospitals, formal gardens, and country clubs. During the post-World War II heyday of the movies, the combined seating of ten elegant and ornate theaters (among them the Rialto, Queen, Arcadia, Savoy, and Majestic) could accommodate up to 15,000 patrons. The lower part of Wilmington's Market Street, down near the train station, lived up to its name, for that was where butchers and grocers sold their wares in open-air stalls to a diverse group of shoppers from the city's neighborhoods—Polish, Italian, Jewish.

Visiting my grandmother, I was aware of the city's physical spaces and sights that seemed alien to me—city sidewalks; a central square adorned with a statue of the local hero, Caesar Rodney, mounted on his horse; public parks with their flower beds; granite steps leading up to public buildings; banks with tellers' windows and post offices with clerks' windows; cavernous movie theaters like the Rialto; and apartment buildings with tile-floor vestibules, cramped-cage elevators, and ill-lit hallways.

As far as I could tell, Wilmington was whiter than Christiana. In keeping with the quasi-southern character of Delaware, the public life of the city remained strictly segregated by race as mandated by a Jim Crow state law passed in 1875, one of the first in the nation. However, segregation meant not that black people were kept apart from whites within certain public places or commercial establishments, but rather that they were barred from entering these places altogether. In the early 1950s, the city's black residents, long relegated to Eastside, a neighborhood of rickety frame dwellings, old factories, and railroad tracks, were organizing to defy the laws that excluded them from local department stores, theaters, and restaurants. The segregated laps of the city's all-white department-store Santas forced black families to travel to the relatively egalitarian Litt Brothers in Philadelphia.[1] As far as I could tell, the city's African American population (at that time 16 percent of the total) was nowhere to be seen on Market Street or in the various, successive neighborhoods inhabited by my grandmother. Occasionally I did see knots of black men waiting for work early in the morning down by the railroad station, and those same men, or men like them, climbing wearily out of the back of a flatbed truck in the same place, at the end of the day. To me, these men represented yet another strange piece of the Wilmington cityscape.

Embodying the faintly exotic Jones-Wilmington family culture was my father's mother. City-bred, thin, and with a frail but enduring elegance, my Jones grandmother always appeared in public, and always welcomed us into whatever tiny apartment she happened to be living in at the time, formally attired and made up—wearing a dress or suit, her face rouged and lipsticked, with huge diamond rings on her fingers, thick gold spangle bracelets on her wrists, and heavy gold clip-ons on her ears. The large brown raised mole on her lower lip gave her a glamorous air, and, of all the women I knew, she went to the beauty parlor most often, keeping her fashionably short steel-gray hair immaculately coifed.

Living in genteel poverty, she seemed to carry remnants of her family's long-lost wealth on her person—now glittering, perfumed, and bejeweled—as if this were a way to preserve precious memories of a privileged girlhood. She presented a striking contrast to my Phelps grandmother, who late in life continued to can her own peaches and beans and maintain a large house in the essentially rural setting of Christiana, and who at home was rarely seen without her full-bib, faded floral-print cotton apron.

The Joneses professed little interest in genealogy. This branch apparently hailed from Virginia originally, and then migrated north to Delaware. An amalgam of German, Scotch-Irish, and Welsh settlers, they possessed no clear-cut ethnic roots. Without the aid of family documents to confirm, deny or expand upon an oral tradition, the Jones history I learned stretched back only to the late nineteenth century. Born in 1891 to a prominent Wilmington businessman, my Jones grandmother had nevertheless been forced to watch helplessly as the family fortunes dwindled precipitously over the course of her lifetime. As a girl she lived the late-Victorian good life, her education finished in 1908 when she took a grand tour of Europe. But when her father died in 1902, the money in the family passed to her mother, who was at a loss about how to manage it, and to her older brother, a dentist who let large sums slip through his fingers. The brother's flourishing practice came to an abrupt halt sometime in the late 1920s when one of his patients suffered a heart attack in the dentist's chair. And his life was marked by other tragedies as well—he suffered from chronic alcoholism, his wife was in and out of Farnhurst, the state institution for the mentally ill, and his sixteen-year-old son died in an auto accident in Wilmington. In contrast, the Phelpses managed to avoid such concentrated pain and suffering by virtue of their great good luck and their collective aversion to high-risk living of any kind.

In 1912 my grandmother would seem to have escaped her mother's faltering household and secure her own future when she married my grandfather, an up-and-coming young man in the Wilmington landscape-contracting business. Their son, who was called by his middle name, my grandmother's maiden name, was born in 1914, and my father was born five years later. Yet by the 1930s this new family too had fallen on hard times. As building ceased in Wilmington during the Great Depression, my grandfather turned to binge drinking, deserting his wife without formally divorcing her, leaving her a "grass widow." She was forced to assume sole responsibility for their two sons. During these years, as a teenager, my father developed his scrappy—some would say combative—temperament, his lifelong disdain for beans as "poor people's food," and his three-pack-a-day cigarette habit.

Walking with my mother down a Wilmington sidewalk in 1944, my father suddenly turned to her and asked, "Did you see the man who just passed us?" It was his father, whom he could not bring himself to acknowledge with even a curt hello. Unlike his brother, my father felt compelled to attend their father's funeral, in 1952; but among the three of them—my father and his mother and brother—none of them appeared to mourn their loss.

My grandmother remained in Wilmington for the rest of her life but moved to a different apartment every couple of years. I never understood what she was searching for—a cheaper place, a nicer place, a bigger place, perhaps. All of them, situated within a few blocks' radius of Wilmington's central city, possessed the same essential features; whether in a four-story apartment building or a two-story townhouse, they were dark, quiet, and suffused with the smell of my grandmother's perfume and cigarette smoke.

Into each new apartment she would stuff the few huge, hulking, mahogany-black pieces of furniture she managed to salvage from her parents' well-appointed home—a bedstead and wardrobe, a floor-length freestanding mirror and a couple of high-backed upholstered wood chairs. I remember sitting on her sofa, drinking Coke from a bottle she had opened with an iron can opener in the shape of a red, green and yellow parrot—the beak was the opener—and reaching for a small wooden box on her coffee table. Balancing the heavy box on my lap I would locate the hidden compartment that held a little key, unlock it, and fish through the collection of postcards she had accumulated during her trip to Europe, marveling at the scenes of wild Sicilian countryside, the piles of human skulls unearthed in Roman catacombs. By this time my grandmother's life was circumscribed by three places—Christiana, Ogletown, and Wilmington. Together they formed a little triangle, one easily traversed in the space of an early Sunday afternoon.

My father was the pivot linking the Phelpses and Joneses. He was bound by an enduring love for his mother and brother but grateful for the uprightness that his wife's extended kin afforded him. When I was growing up in the 1950s, he and my mother adopted a strategy that met with the unstated but no doubt heartfelt approval of all concerned—the Phelps and Jones aunts, uncles, and cousins should never find themselves in the same place at the same time.

My Jones grandmother was the single exception that proved the rule. Well into her seventies, she continued to work at a fashionable downtown Wilmington department store, Kennards, where she sold ladies' coats in the company of other women her age. Periodically Phelps aunts and older cousins would rely on her discerning eye to help them pick out a winter coat, and when they spoke of her they spoke of her fondly, and used her nickname, Tish. They admired her sense of style and appreciated her discreet demeanor. Then too, every Christmas eve she would come to our house for dinner and later in the evening accompany us to church, the province of Phelps-es. Like the spectacle of the lighted candles held aloft during the end of the service, when the congregation joined in singing "Joy to the World," the sight of my grandmother in such close proximity to my mother's family struck me as wonderful but a little dangerous, a miracle that occurred only once a year.

For her part, my mother remained stoic during her encounters with Jonesdom because she was in love with my father. Moreover, she and everyone else knew that her own extended family trumped my father's in the Sunday afternoon sweepstakes, the prize that she fervently prayed would shape the character of her own children. Throughout the year, regardless of the weather, the Phelps aunts, uncles and cousins made their weekly pilgrimage to my grandmother's colonial-style house on East Main Street, a visit that took place after the noontime Sunday dinner and lasted until the late afternoon. They came, family by family, in their Plymouths, Dodges, and Chevrolets, some still in Sunday finery.

The extended family presented itself as a walking advertisement of middle-class postwar family life. By 1957, four families had among them eleven children (three had three, one had two), ranging in ages from eighteen, the oldest, a girl, to one, the youngest, a boy (my younger brother). Each family had one child born within two years of me (that is, between 1947 and 1949). Two were a year older, one was a year younger, one was a boy, two were girls. The four of us were fast friends, our closeness insulated from the petty jealousies and rivalries that often rocked schoolyard friendships.

On Sunday afternoons, depending on the time of year, the cousins might play a game of croquet on my grandmother's front lawn, swim in the pond behind our house, or explore the woods as far as an afternoon walk would take us. If they stayed late enough, until twilight, we could use the Ball canning jars we found in my grandmother's kitchen to catch fireflies, using the makeshift lanterns to illuminate the recessed chambers at the base of the two huge blue spruce trees in her front yard. When they left for home, the four families did not have far to go—to Newark, to Stanton, to Newport—the latter two towns also located on the banks of the Christina River on its way to Wilmington.

My mother was the daughter of two natives of Massachusetts, and their lineage, inscribed in a variety of handwritten documents handed down through the generations, provided fodder for Sunday afternoon conversations. The Phelpses were aware of the fact that they went way back. My grandfather's family traced its roots in this country back to 1630, when William Phelps arrived on the *Mary and John* with others who were the original settlers of the Massachusetts Bay Colony. By 1637 William Phelps had left Boston and migrated south to help found the town of Windsor, Connecticut; he presided over the General Court that declared war on the Pequot Indians that year. A descendant of William's, Henry Arthur Phelps, my grandfather, was born in 1875, and grew up in Northampton, Massachusetts. A few years after his father died in 1886, he finished high school and went to work to help support his sister and mother who made a living as a seamstress and laundress. He met my grandmother one day when he was delivering a load of finished laundry to one of the housekeeping units at Smith College, where she was a student. At the time, their courtship was considered quite shocking—the well-to-do girls at Smith were not supposed to socialize with boys, especially poor boys, from the town. Moreover my grandmother's parents took great pride in their daughter's accomplishments—she had attended Classical High School in Worcester, Massachusetts, and then majored in Greek and Latin at college—and they expected great things from her. (What this meant in late nineteenth-century terms I am not certain—a faculty position at her alma mater perhaps?) But after graduation she disappointed them by teaching classical languages for a year and a half at the high school in nearby Shrewsbury, and then quitting at Christmastime to marry my grandfather. She devoted the rest of her life to raising their family. Their children went on to graduate from a variety of colleges—Smith, Lafayette, Beacom Business College in Wilmington, the University of Delaware.

My grandfather had managed to redeem himself in the eyes of his new in-laws to some extent by learning civil engineering through a correspondence course and eventually finding steady work, if not a settled existence, as a land surveyor. For many years he was an employee of coal mining companies and railroad operators in the mountains, from the Pennsylvania Alleghanies to the Blue Ridge of Kentucky. His eight children were born in five different states—Massachusetts, Pennsylvania, Kentucky, West Virginia, and Virginia.

I detected echoes of this story in the courtship and marriage of my own parents—the boy from humble circumstances marries the brainy college graduate and, making up in raw intelligence what he lacks in formal education, insures that she will not have to work outside the home. In both my grandparents' and parents' households, a middle-class rectitude held sway, with both men, my grandfather and my father, achieving a hard-won respectability. In contrast, my mother and her mother had claimed that respectability as their birthright.

My father graduated from Wilmington High School in 1937, and then combined a job in a DuPont Company mailroom with night classes at the University of Pennsylvania's Wharton School of Business in Philadelphia, earning the title (if not degree) of "Wharton Evening Undergraduate" in 1941. My parents were introduced to each other on the boardwalk at Rehoboth Beach in southern Delaware on Labor Day of that year. In December he enlisted in the service, and began basic training three months later.

My mother had graduated from Newark High School and entered the University of Delaware in 1936. There she majored in English and wrote a senior thesis on the southern writer Ellen Glasgow. After finishing college she took a job in the advertising department of the DuPont Company, a position she held until 1943 when she became the editor of RCA Victor's company newsletter and embarked on a rather glamorous, if brief, bachelorette existence in Philadelphia.

Meanwhile, as a newly inducted member of the United States Air Force, my father followed a circuitous path that would eventually take him to the South Pacific. While working in a mailroom in a DuPont office building in Wilmington, he had acquired a civilian pilot's license on weekends and during his lunch hour at nearby

Ballanca Airport in New Castle. His kindly supervisor looked the other way when he returned to work late in the afternoon every day. Before the war he took only one person, other than a flight instructor, up in the air with him—his own mother, who agreed to go after her other son flatly refused a similar invitation.

My father's first wartime assignment was pilot training school in Nashville. There, during his final, airborne examination he was presented with a life-or-death problem: Fuel is running low: Should you proceed to your destination or return to base? He made the wrong choice, whatever it was, and was dispatched to Biloxi, Mississippi, to study radio operations. He either could not or would not learn Morse code quickly enough, and spent time in other air bases in Colorado, North Dakota, and California before receiving his final assignment of the war in the fall of 1944—Twentieth Air Force, 498 Bomber Group, based on the island of Saipan. He took advantage of his last furlough in 1944 to propose to his girlfriend in his mother's living room. The bride-to-be had already made up her mind and so said yes.

My father was a technical sergeant on a B-29 (the so-called "Superfortress") and served as Central Fire Control ("Top Gun") on the top of the plane. Through an intercom he radioed to the tail gunners below and directed their machine-gun fire to oncoming targets in the air. He and the other crew members successfully completed their quota of thirty bombing missions, mostly raids over Japanese cities.

During the last fifteen months or so of the war, the Twentieth had grown from 94 aircraft and 143 crews to over one thousand aircraft and 1,378 crews of ten men each. Years later a history of the Twentieth would chronicle its achievements in the form of statistics, cold-blooded testimony about the death and destruction my father saw and helped wreak during his year in Saipan: 65 principal cities obliterated or severely damaged; 602 major war factories destroyed; 1,250,000 tons of shipping sunk by aerial mines; 83 percent of oil refinery production and 75 percent of aircraft engine production destroyed; 2,300,000 homes leveled; 330,000 men, women, and children killed and 476,000 wounded; 8,500,000 people rendered homeless and 21,000,000 displaced.[2] Fatalities for the Twentieth numbered 3,000 men. Viewed from this perspective, the atomic bombs represented a gruesome climax to, and not a radical departure from, the earlier devastation produced by conventional air raids. My father survived but, like many other veterans of this generation I have since learned, he never told us war stories.

In college I read Joseph Heller's *Catch-22* without the slightest sense that the book might provide some clues to my father's reticence about the war. On its return from one bombing mission, his plane had had to make an emergency landing on a deserted island. On another mission he was wounded by enemy gunfire and later awarded an oak-leaf cluster. He had been hit in the rear—not the plane's rear end but his own—and was a bit embarrassed about the inglorious and minor nature of the wound, so he never mentioned the medal to us. Only a few artifacts scattered around the house testified to the danger he had endured every day for almost a year—a photograph taken from his plane of snow-covered Mount Fuji, now on the wall over his desk in the den; his flight jacket, embossed with the fire-spouting dragon of the Twentieth, hanging in an upstairs bedroom closet; a yearbook with pictures of his plane, the *Lady Mary Anna,* upon which was painted a picture of the lady herself—a high-heeled, scantily clad, curvaceous figure that graced the side of the aircraft. (Other planes in his bomber group had slightly more provocative names: *Urgin Virgin, Supine Sue, Sweet Thing, Teaser.*) Apparently his stint on Saipan had been made more bearable by the fact that he respected all of his crewmates and greatly admired his commander, a daredevil who went about as far as he could in defying his superiors without being court-martialed. My father had within him that same kind of spirit, though he lacked the kind of life-work that would have allowed him to make use of it.

My parents saw each other sporadically early in their courtship, and then they had to keep the flame alive through letters and my father's infrequent furloughs. At some point he informed my mother that he wanted to get married within two weeks of his discharge. He was mustered out of the service on September 2, 1945, and they were married in the Christiana Presbyterian Church followed by a reception at my grandparents' house thirteen days later. Though not tall, they both possessed movie-star good looks—my father slim, handsome, with the twinkling blue eyes that were his distinguishing feature; my mother with wavy, shoulder-length dark hair and a beatific smile. By the time of their wedding my parents had spent a total of only a few full days in each other's company, but theirs was a romantic and enduring marriage. Over the next half century their relationship would serve as a testament to the integrity of so many other marriages forged on the fly, in the crucible of war.

In 1950, accepting my grandfather's gift of a parcel of land next to his house in Christiana, my parents settled in Phelps territory, which was a state of mind as much as a place. My father never took a plane up again. However, on occasion he did take his family out to Sunday dinner at the New Castle County airport restaurant, a few minutes east on Route 13. By that time, for my mother, brothers, and me, the airfield was a site of domesticity, not feats of daring.

The Phelpses regretted leaving New England, but they made a home for themselves in this nondescript Delaware town. In the absence of any Congregational churches in the area, they had had to make do with a small Presbyterian congregation that was barely surviving. We stayed in touch with close relatives in Massachusetts and, in my grandparent's living room, copies of the *Farmer's Almanac* were scattered among issues of *Reader's Digest* and *Presbyterian Life*. Virtually all of my grandparents' personal habits and tastes—their diets, their frugality, their household-industrial skills, their conservative style of speech and clothing—were hailed as distinctive "Yankee" traits, not so much a legacy of a bygone era as a statement about who we were as a family, in the 1950s, in alien territory, the Border State of Delaware.

The collective Phelps family persona revealed itself most forcefully in the form of a complacent, midlevel bureaucratic ethos. It would be unfair to suggest that the men of the family lacked entrepreneurial drive or vision. Back in Worcester, my grandmother's two brothers had owned their own businesses—a butcher shop and a jewelry store, respectively—and in Delaware her husband was operating his own sand and gravel business by the 1930s. Yet my grandfather had been almost principled in his lack of ambition. Throughout his career, first as contract worker and then as the owner of a small business, he charged for expenses and made only a small profit, choosing not to cash in on his technical expertise. One of my uncles-by-marriage, together with his brother, operated a busy appliance store in Newport. Nevertheless, my other Phelps uncles were like my father—employees, whether of DuPont or the U.S. Postal Service, and not businessmen.

After the war, my father had been assigned to the General Services/Supplies division of DuPont, and later worked in production, then personnel, and then accounting. His job provided him with little intrinsic satisfaction, and his bosses seemed determined not to take advantage of his considerable talents and drive. Still, for him, and for the extended Phelps family as a whole, a steady salary yielded a way of life that afforded its own comfortable satisfactions. In contrast, the Joneses inclined toward gambling with life-choices, and especially livelihoods. My Jones grandfather had invested heavily in a landscape-contracting business that failed, but his son my uncle invested heavily in the same kind of business and succeeded with the help of state contracts and some efficient foremen.

My father and his brother followed quite different career paths, but they shared a strong bond forged first on the tough streets of their childhood in Wilmington and then reinforced by their unheralded heroism during the war. While my father was positioned atop a bomber shooting down Japanese kamikazes, his brother (who eventually attained the rank of major) was part of the 82nd Airborne 504th Parachute Regiment, paratrooping into France and Italy, making one hundred jumps and surviving enemy fire on several occasions. Each winter in the 1950s, the two of them would take a weeklong car trip to Maine, where they would freeze together in an unheated cabin and go through the motions of hunting for deer and bear. All of us understood these excursions had less to do with putting venison on the Joneses' tables and more to do with recapturing a bit of masculine bravado now that their families and responsibilities were growing.

If the Joneses were edgy and a tad unpredictable, the Phelpses were safe, even staid, as revealed by their routine get-togethers. Later, I would come to think of Sunday afternoons next door at my Phelps grandmother's house (my grandfather died in 1953) not only in terms of what we did, but also in terms of what we did not do—eat for one thing. Neither my grandmother nor the unmarried daughter who lived with her ever prepared so much as a cup of tea or coffee on Sunday afternoon, nor did the guests ever brazenly dare to help themselves to anything. In fact, no one ventured into the kitchen for any reason; that room was the site of meal preparation three times a day, not the source of snacks or the place for idle chitchat. The cousins drew freely from the long-stemmed pewter candy dish in the hallway off the living room, picking through the mound of Mary Janes, gumdrops, Hershey's Crackles, and jelly beans. For real sustenance, however, they were forced to forage in my father's vegetable garden. Lacking that option most of the year, they had to rely on my good graces to spirit cookies out of my own kitchen. I never associated any particular food with my extended family.

Sunday afternoons also lacked outsiders of any kind—no friends of cousins or out-of-town visitors disrupted the carefully calibrated harmony of this Sabbath-day family ritual. In contrast to the decade before and the one after, the 1950s, for the Phelpses as a whole, was a time undisturbed by early deaths or deaths from unnatural causes. My grandfather passed away at the age of 78, and my cousin, who suffered from cystic fibrosis, lived an exceptionally long life for one so afflicted, well into his twenties. He died in 1972. We endured no immediate family crises arising from mental illness, divorce, substance abuse, or addiction of any kind—whether to gambling, shopping or sex. I suspect that few extended families could boast of such a placid infrastructure, bolstered by members of such uniformly even personalities.

And so it was the Phelpses who set the high standard for family comportment that prevailed in my own house next door. Characteristically, if somewhat fantastically, during these Sunday afternoon get-togethers there were no angry words or arguments, no heated disagreements about politics or personalities, no invective or criticism—implied or direct—of persons present. The aunts loved to laugh and tell stories at their own expense, but they contributed few if any colorful linguistic turns to these conversations. They did offer a few family epigrams, though: On the relative discomfort caused by the weather in the summer and winter, it was agreed that the cold was preferable because you could always pile on more layers, while in the heat of the summer there was a limit to what you could take off. As children we were supposed to remain ignorant of the age of any adult; but to the prying question of a cousin, an aunt might reply that she was as old as her tongue and a little older than her teeth. While other families cultivated colorful insults that they flung at each other on a regular basis, the Phelps aunts had no use for these forms of rhetorical creativity.

The aunts expressed dismay in gently funny ways, invoking little epithets that harkened back to the original obscenities they were meant to replace. Thus instead of "Jesus!" I heard: "Jiminy Cricket," "gee" (or "gee whiz" or "gee whillikers"), "jeepers," and "jumping Jehosephat"; and, in place of "shit" I heard: "shucks" and "shoot." "Darn" and "heck" were obvious well-worn stand-ins. "Oh my word" was the equivalent of "oh my God," and "good night," "good grief," and "good heavens" all-purpose exclamations of surprise. Among the extended clan, my father was the only one to use the genuine articles whenever he swore, though never of course in the presence of anyone from his wife's family; those were Jones words.

In the absence of bruising confrontations among individuals who happened to be related by blood or marriage, these Sunday afternoons yielded a scripted, soothing affirmation of the way this particular family perceived itself. Indeed, the deeper domestic politics of Phelps family life remained a mystery to me throughout much of this period. For example, by the 1950s, the jealousy that the aunts directed toward my mother as the petted youngest of the family had dissipated into jokes (mostly lighthearted) about her good fortune in avoiding both hand-me-down dresses and the kinds of arduous manual labor that a family of ten with modest resources entailed. Later I would learn a little about the rivalries that had—predictably—characterized life in a large family. Indeed, the single brother and his seven younger sisters had shared among themselves two distinct family experiences. The oldest siblings remembered helping their parents to scrimp and save to make ends meet, contributing to the household by working in the summer and after school as they moved from one rented house to another. In contrast, my mother the youngest remembered more comfortable times, a carefree childhood, one relatively devoid of money worries.

On Sunday afternoons the aunts reminisced about life in a big family, their stories harmless and at times self-mocking. Apparently my mother and her next-oldest sister had carried on a long-running, if mostly good-natured, feud, the two of them rivals for my no-doubt-harried grandmother's attention. One day in the kitchen, my mother threw a jar of mustard and managed to hit her target—her sister's forehead—causing an ugly bruise, as well as many tears on both sides. I am fairly certain that that was the last (and probably the first) instance of violence to be perpetrated by my mother on another human being. But when I was growing up, strong feelings of all kinds lay deep under the surface of Sunday afternoons.

Also missing from these gatherings were expressions of historic resentments focused on a particular group. Other families might have legitimate grievances against Protestants, Gentiles, the English or white people; but the Phelpses, prideful of their long and honorable New England heritage, represented a group more resented than resentful. This would change only late in the decade, when black protesters in the South came into view on the evening TV news, prompting cranky, if muted, discussions of a poor, benighted segment of the population that wanted too much too fast. Before this, however, family life assumed the tone of smug sanctimony. We seemed to be immune to tragedy, our judgmental stance in the world a result of, and testimony to, our collective self-righteousness.

Each week the grown-ups clustered in my grandmother's living room, a large room with dark rugs on the floor and a baby grand piano off in the corner. Their conversation distracted only infrequently—for example, by a Phillies game on TV in the summer—my aunts held forth. More often than not their only brother receded—eagerly, I could tell even then—into the background. The oldest of the family, he received dispensation to sit out of the way and read the Sunday newspaper or *Newsweek* magazine, ignoring (or unaware of) any mention of his name in the course of the conversation. For their part, my three uncles-by-marriage, all tall, with glasses and good natures, seemed to take pleasure in the predictable Sunday routine presided over by their wives and sisters-in-law. With one of them, my only childless uncle in the environs of Christiana, I replayed over and over again our favorite conversation—speculation about where we might find "the end of the counting," an idea that alternately fascinated and terrified me. But by and large these afternoons belonged to the women, my aunts and mother and their mother.

My grandmother occupied the literal and figurative center, sitting in a high-backed easy chair, with a sturdy wooden tray table in front of her. This was the place where she sat every day of the week and worked word puzzles of all kinds—crosswords, quote acrostics, and cryptograms. She embraced the challenge of puzzles as a respite from the mind-numbing routine of housework. Indeed, to the end of her life her mind remained as sharp as the pencil she wielded in her bony, liver-spotted hand. Though her days as a classical scholar were long past, she still possessed a killer vocabulary.

These Sunday afternoon discussions flowed easily through three or four narrow and wholly anticipated channels. The family core hashed over the church service they had attended that morning: the choice of hymns (Weren't parts of that last one too high for all but the choir soloist to reach? Hadn't we sung "Amazing Grace" just a couple of weeks before?); the sporadic or ongoing health problems of those in attendance; and the sermon—not so much its substance but its length, either too long or too short. Governance of the church also received a disproportionate amount of attention, with the upcoming elections of trustees and elders prompting a great deal of speculation and plans for informal politicking.

The town of Christiana itself, replete with a modest but clearly identifiable mix of Methodists and Southerners (these categories overlapping with the laboring classes and the sinners) afforded endless material for discussion. As the local correspondent for the Newark *Post*, my mother was the official repository of townspeople's comings and goings. For her weekly "Christiana Calling" column she made it her business to know who was visiting whom, who had had a new baby, who had attended what meeting. Each Sunday evening she began to work the phone, hunting for news so that she could meet her Monday-afternoon deadline: "Sunday visitors at the home of Mr. and Mrs. Olan Cleaver were Mr. and Mrs. Albert Stephenson of Ferris Road and Mr. and Mrs. Russell Cleaver of Middletown" (this in a December, 1954, issue of the *Post*). In the absence of newsworthy activities sponsored by the white school and the two white churches; by the Cub Scouts, Boy Scouts, Explorers, Brownies or Girl Scouts; or by the firehouse or its Ladies Auxiliary, my mother used her own family as filler—a visit from her out-of-town sister ("Mrs. Harkins is the former Katherine Phelps"), my brother's tonsillectomy. In the July 2, 1959, issue, I was highlighted in two consecutive paragraphs: as a player in "a modern adaptation of the parable of the Good Samaritan" at the Presbyterian Church, and as host of a "hot dog roast" enjoyed by the junior class of the Christiana Community Bible School. Intensely interested in the rhythms of Christiana life, my aunts appreciated their youngest sister as both scribe and messenger of town happenings, roles that elevated her authority within the realm of the Phelps-family folk culture.

Town matters, the fortunes of the Phillies baseball team and the genius of Robin Roberts and Richie Ashburn, the cut of a cousin's new school band uniform, the weather and the sweetness of the late-summer's corn—all of these things served as the white noise of Sunday afternoon gatherings. More revealing, however, were the patterns of family interaction that relied by turns on the self-deprecation and the self-indulgence of the participants. The aunts loved to poke fun at each other and themselves, recounting occurrences both ordinary and startling:

Aunt One: Did anybody notice? On the steps outside of church this morning I felt the elastic in my slip waistband snap. I let the slip fall to the ground, and just stepped right out of it, put it in my purse, and kept on going!
All aunts in unison: No!
Aunt One: What was I supposed to do—stand there with it hanging around my ankles, waiting for [the minister] to pick it up and give it to me?
[convulsive laughter]

Or:

Aunt One: It was so windy today that my hat blew off my head and I was worried that my hair was going to blow away at the same time [this observation no doubt for the benefit of the cousins in attendance].
Aunt Two: Putting your hair back on your head would have been a problem.
Aunt Three: She would have had to paste it on.
Aunt Four: Scotch tape would have been less messy.
Aunt One: I'm glad nobody is mentioning a staple gun in this discussion!
[peals of laughter]

While these conversations were taking place, the aunts might engage in the Combing of the Hair. It was common knowledge that all Phelps women liked to have their hair combed, and once in a while one would sit on the living room floor while one of the others combed her hair. Then they would switch places. Of course only sisters could provide this kind of homoerotic service for each other in my grandmother's living room on Sunday afternoons. The husbands sat and watched.

Although the cousins and I drifted in and out of these gatherings, rarely did the aunts' voices drop to a whisper, and rarely did the grown-ups pause in mid-sentence out of deference to our innocent ears. I knew that they restrained themselves from expressing disapproval of a wide variety of individuals—family, friends, preachers, elected officials—and exchanging bits of salacious gossip—about drunken fights and unwed mothers in the town—until they could talk to each other on the telephone during the week. Sunday afternoons were reserved for public displays of clan solidarity as defined by the aunt-archy.

As for my brothers and me, our last name was Jones but it was always clear that geography and temperament decreed that we must consider ourselves Phelpses first and foremost. Not surprisingly, then, holiday celebrations revolved around my grandmother next door, and we moved to the Phelps-based rhythms of church and Sunday School on Sunday, choir practice on Tuesday night, with an arduous schedule of official church and school meetings for my parents scattered throughout the week. It was my Phelps cousins who came to my house to help me celebrate my birthday with Hawaiian Punch and homemade cake (my mother's special "Black Magic" recipe with crunchy boiled "seven-minute" icing). They were the ones who swam with us in the pond on lazy summer afternoons, and their mothers helped to care for me and my brothers whenever the occasion arose.

Yet fairness (not to mention my father's sanity) decreed that we must every once in a while forego the placid pleasures of a Sunday afternoon in Christiana in favor of some time with the Joneses. In the car on the way to Ogletown, a ten-minute trip, I would try to brace myself for the sensory overload that awaited me at the end of the ride.

My uncle's house, a rambling nineteenth-century stucco-and-stone farmhouse with thick walls and a wide front porch, sat back from the road, shielded by a tall hedge of sycamore trees. Behind the house was a low-lying building the shape of a large chicken coop, and not far from that was the barn, a huge, four-story wooden structure with stalls for the horses on the ground floor and a hayloft above. A field for the horses, sheep, goats, and cows stretched behind this collection of buildings, a gateway of sorts to the thick woods that lay beyond.

My aunt and uncle enjoyed entertaining small groups of friends and relatives these Sunday afternoons, and in their living room the Lord's Day was awash in alcohol. Predictably, the Joneses enforced the general principle that children should be neither seen nor heard. The fact that they had four children, instead of the sacred three enshrined by contemporary Phelps mores, struck me as excessive. The fact that my four cousins, my brothers, and I were all banished from the living room, and usually from the house itself, struck me as ungenerous at best. We spent most of our time outdoors or in the outbuildings.

Only on rainy days were we permitted to stay in the kitchen or the rooms upstairs, all places that smelled like dogs. And no wonder: The household boasted an impressive assortment of them—white and brown beagles, a ghost-grey weimaraner, a brindle-colored mastiff, a yellow Great Dane, and a tiny creature named Tootsie, part Chihuahua, part rat terrier. The big dogs loomed as large as small horses (the Dane weighed 180 pounds), and all of them had the run of the house, petted and fussed over like lapdogs. Accustomed to more reasonably sized cats and dogs, I thought of these creatures not so much as pets as strange boarders that cohabited with my cousins, creatures that occupied a position of relative privilege within this odd family. In the winter, while we braved the Sunday-afternoon cold, the dogs got to stay inside.

Still, we had no difficulty amusing ourselves in and around the farm, a place that was part zoo, part three-ring circus, part house of horrors, part boot-camp-for-boys. With nothing better to do, my four cousins played the role of solicitous hosts and entertained us in their peculiar way. It was on my uncle's long, downward sloping driveway that I learned to ride a bike one afternoon. My cousins put me on a bike, gave me a good push, and cheered me on as, drawn like a moth to a light, a nail to a magnet, I time after time crashed into the single tree on the side of the driveway. But I did learn to ride a bike.

On any particular afternoon, it was only a matter of time before we found our way to the barn. My own favorite diversion was balancing precariously on a side beam of the hayloft and, clutching a coarsely braided rope, leaping into the void. The rope burned my hands, and I learned the hard way that it was impossible to steer myself one way or another in midair. If I was lucky, I fell safely into a pile of hay, emerging gasping for breath, eyes stinging from dirt and dust, ready to scramble up and do it again. Sometimes though I would crash onto the wooden plank floor, lying there with the wind knocked out of me, my cousins duly appreciative of my daring.

A tour of the low-lying outbuilding yielded other delights—giant freezers used to store the beef from my uncle's slaughtered cows; a variety of old furniture, bicycles, farm implements, and cages. These last items were filled with wild animals *du jour*—baby squirrels, possums, skunks, and raccoons adopted by the family. The Joneses took their animals seriously; for example, they went to the trouble of having the skunks descented by the farm's veterinarian, an operation performed outside, and not inside, his hospital. More intriguing was the array of exotica imported from around the world—a spider monkey and a kinkajou for example. A native of Central America, the kinkajou was a brown, furry animal, with a thick tail longer than the length of its body. I wondered how this strange thing, presumably born in a tropical rain forest, survived longer than a day or two in a cage in a dank storage room on my uncle's farm.

My uncle loved animals of all kinds. In fact, he first attracted the attention of his future wife by strolling down a Wilmington sidewalk one day with a pet raccoon perched on his shoulder. However, conventional wisdom held that he took things too far when he arranged for two American buffalo, christened Samson and Delilah, to be delivered to Ogletown in the mid-1950s. Within a few days of their arrival, late at night by truck, they proceeded to break out of their fence and terrorize the neighbors. The new pen built to contain them was so gigantic it used telephone poles for corner posts.

The buffalo provided my uncle's family with a certain amount of celebrity among outsiders, a certain amount of notoriety among the neighbors. Driving by on the road that ran in front of his house, curiosity seekers would slow down to get a glimpse of the huge beasts morosely grazing on the grass of the front lawn. If the passersby stopped to get a better look they might be in for a shock: More than one innocent family was startled by the appearance of my uncle's pet monkey, which would jump into the front seat through the window on the driver's side, grab the car keys out of the ignition and scurry to present them as a trophy to his owner, who was always greatly amused by this feat.

Languishing in the mild mid-Atlantic weather, the buffalo met with an untimely demise after a year and a half, succumbing to the shock of—well, any number of things. Years later my oldest Jones cousin (not surprisingly he had become a veterinarian) told me that in all probability the buffalo had died from parasites. Unlike their natural habitat on the Great Plains, my uncle's front yard failed to provide sufficient space for the combined activity of eating and defecating.

It was likely the animals were also agitated by the trains that roared by several times a day. Running along the border of my uncle's property, within fifty feet or so of his house, was a major freight route between Wilmington and Baltimore. Hoboes riding the rails routinely made an appearance at the back door; the family fed them and they went on their way. A couple of times every afternoon a train would come by, shaking the house to its foundations and, in anticipation of the nearby railroad crossing, blowing a whistle that could be heard as far as Newark, or so it seemed.

My cousins had become so accustomed to the trains that they were oblivious, but my brothers and I would stand by the side of the tracks and wave to the men in the engine and the caboose, so close we could feel the backdraft as the train sped by, just a misstep or two away from a severed limb. In fact, one of my cousins once had a brush with death, when the horse he was riding near the house suddenly and inexplicably bolted onto the tracks before an oncoming train. My cousin fell off in the nick of time, and the horse managed to make it to the other side; but that kind of scare seemed to be routine part of what we today might call the Jones family "lifestyle."

On any Sunday, various displays of physicality were *de rigueur,* for my cousins lived in a daredevil world with features drawn from military basic training. Haircuts told a larger story: We all bore a general family resemblance to each other, but the home-shorn Jones boys were notable for their recruit-style buzz cuts, their hair so short absolutely nothing was left to comb. (My mother's insistence that the barber leave enough on top of my brothers' heads so that they could slick down a little bit with water therefore represented a modest gesture of defiance on her part.) Whenever we were around, at least, the four amused themselves by engaging in mock battles and testing the limits of their own endurance, no doubt in an effort to show off in front of their schoolbookish kinfolk. In the woods, with my brothers and me fulfilling our appointed role as disapproving but gawking bystanders, they fought with swords made from tree branches, and wrestled each other to the ground. They affirmed their bond as brothers by tormenting each other. The first one to cry was the loser, a sissy. A lesser size and a younger age offered no excuse; the rougher the play, the better the play.

Observing these strange performances, my brothers and I remained self-conscious of the fact that we lived the soft life. We did our homework and sang in the junior choir at church. We teased and badgered each other, but refrained from fisticuffs. Our weekly allowances rewarded us for setting the dinner table and pulling weeds in the garden. In contrast, during the week after school and on Saturdays, my uncle routinely put his sons to work for his business. On one occasion the four boys, aged eight to seventeen, were sent to work at a job at Delaware State Hospital for the mentally ill. They had to help unload three tractor-trucks full of sod and then lay the grass on the grounds in two days. After it started to rain heavily, their own duties intensified when several of my uncle's employees quit in disgust. Routinely, the boys were paid 10 cents an hour to work in their father's tree nursery, digging up trees and wrapping them in burlap, a task facilitated only by levers and pulleys in the days before backhoes and cranes.

And too, it was my two oldest Jones cousins, and not my brothers, who accompanied my uncle and father on one of their hellish forays into the backwoods of Maine. Riding facing backwards in the third seat of a stationwagon for fourteen straight hours, inhaling great billows of cigarette smoke from my father in front, only to arrive at a primitive God-forsaken cabin and endure five days of misery, their feet literally sticking to the floor each morning it was so cold, the two of them managed to survive this peculiar Jones rite of passage. Meanwhile, no doubt, their pantywaist cousins were sprawled out on the living room floor watching Mighty Mouse cartoons.

At the end of a Sunday afternoon, covered with straw, our shoes stinking from the cow pods that littered the pasture, hungry and thirsty, my brothers and I made our way back into the main house to throw ourselves on the mercy of our parents. It was then that we might catch a glimpse of Turner (no one ever used his first name), a grizzled, elderly black man who lived in a small room off the kitchen and worked as a general family retainer, responsible for everything from gardening to baby-sitting. Turner liked to preach to the boys; his favorite book of the Bible was Revelation, but his warnings of impending doom had no discernible impact upon his restless listeners. Wending our way to the living room, we were bound to smell tobacco smoke competing with the smell of the dogs, and hear my uncle laughing at one of his own jokes.

Sometimes the joke came at my grandmother's expense. The grown-up equivalent of the horseplay in the woods was my uncle's perverse delight in teasing my grandmother and making her weep, softly but surely. In response to some offhand comment that was more silly than hurtful—We're moving out of the state, Mother, I forgot to tell you—her eyes would well up with tears and she would bite her lower lip and plead, Oh dear no, a cue for him to roar even louder.

I knew from even the little I overheard that the substance and patterns of Jones-talk deviated significantly from its Sunday afternoon Phelps equivalent. My Jones aunt and uncle belonged to no church, and for this reason the huge, ancient leather-bound Jones family Bible that remained in our possession seemed to me to be an oxymoronic heirloom. My father and his brother, in contrast to my mother and her sisters, dominated the conversation. The two of them might discuss local politics, or the latest fiendish plot concocted by the state highway department to pave over all of New Castle County. My aunt was caught up in the Newark social scene, modest though it was, a topic that my mother tolerated with only the greatest difficulty. Once in a while the skeletons rattling around in the Jones-family closet would pop out in the course of the discussion. And too, in contrast to Phelps patterns of discourse, the Joneses directed pointed comments toward each other, putting into play verbs I never associated with my mother's family—criticizing, haranguing, ridiculing, berating. In any case, it seemed to me, the Joneses lived rather large.

When my brothers and I appeared, cowering in the doorway of the living room, my uncle would be there, a gin and tonic in one hand, a glint in his eyes and an ear-to-ear grin on his face. The sight of us would prompt a hearty acknowledgement (I would hardly call it a welcome): "Had enough, kids? All the cows milked, all the horses rubbed down? The raccoons fed and the barn stalls cleaned out? No? Why not, then, you lazy bums? If you didn't worry so much about your homework, and got outside and did an honest day's work, you could earn your keep! Ha Ha Ha!"

My uncle's fond farewell to his brother might consist of a clap on my father's back, and the solemn advice, "Don't forget what I told you Albert: Go deep, always go deep!" The look on my mother's face helped me to translate this remark: He was speaking of the unspeakable in mixed company, a feat that took my breath away and served as a fitting end to our Sunday afternoon excursion through Jones territory.

The contrasts between the Phelps and the Jones Sunday afternoons notwithstanding, I now suspect that both families were marked by the losses they had suffered as much as by the way they lived their lives then. The squandered Jones family fortune bespoke a luxurious past in large, graceful homes along the tree-lined streets of Wilmington. For their part, the Phelpses could hardly help but lament their displacement from New England, and their exile to a pathetic little town that lacked all sense of tradition and history. Yet Christiana was a fitting place for these two genealogies to converge. And as it turned out, in the Kingdom of the Phelpses, I was a closet Jones.

2

Christiana Bridge

Later in life, when I felt compelled to locate myself in the wider world, I realized that I grew up in a place that was neither here nor there. To the north of the crossroads called Christiana lay the rolling hills of DuPont country, the manicured suburbs home to company executives and chemists. To the south lay the coastal plain, the Delmarva Peninsula, a land of chicken coops and truck farms. During the 1950s Delaware possessed two opposing state symbols. One was "Red Hannah" the whipping post, a relic still used in prison court-yards throughout all three counties; and the other was the sideways, elongated oval logo of the DuPont Company, synonymous with "Better Living Through Chemistry." Both of these Delaware identities were noteworthy, one pointing toward the state's slave past, the other toward the region's high-tech future. And yet the town of Christiana could lay claim to neither of them.

We did not realize it at the time, but in the 1950s the town was in an historic slough, a lull, to put it charitably. A sweeping perspective, one that encompasses all of Christiana's recorded history, reveals alternate cycles of growth, decline, and revitalization. Yet I belonged to a generation living at the intersection of nothing in particular. The place existed as a geographical site, to be sure, but as a community we showed no capacity, or inclination, to imagine what things were like long ago, or to aspire to something different in the future.

Though we know little about the earliest inhabitants of the site now called Christiana, the general region was settled as many as one thousand years before the first Europeans arrived in the seventeenth century. Located just a few miles west of the Delaware River, and eighty miles north of the confluence of that river and the ocean, the area was (and is) part of the Atlantic Flyway, a seasonal migration route for hundreds of thousands of birds. The Indians who lived there called themselves the Leni-Lenape, which meant, in their language, *real men,* and they were part of a larger group scattered

42

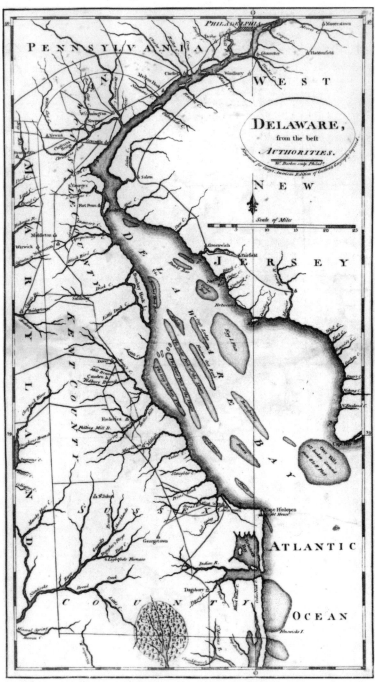

Delaware, From the Best Authorities (Philadelphia: M. Carey, 1795). University of Delaware Library, Newark, Delaware.

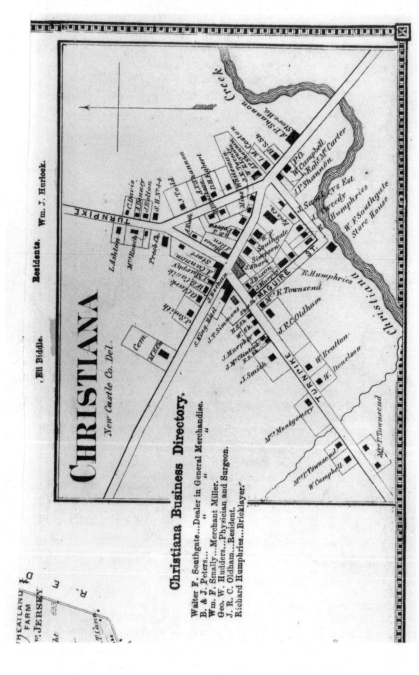

Town of Christiana from D. G. Beers' *Atlas of the State of Delaware* (Philadelphia: Pomeroy and Beers, 1868). University of Delaware Library, Newark, Delaware.

through what is now New Jersey and eastern Pennsylvania as well as Delaware.[1] Wedged between the Iroquois Nation of the north (centered in what is now New York state) and the Algonquian Confederacy to the south (in Virginia), the Leni-Lenape lived in small villages and for many generations managed to avoid entangling alliances with either of their more powerful neighbors. Their labor patterns were similar to those of other groups on the eastern seaboard; the men hunted and fished and the women tended crops, cooked, and cared for the children.[2]

By the early seventeenth century, the appearance of European invaders had alternately provoked and exacerbated inter-Indian rivalries. The Delaware Indians, as they came to be called by the English, found themselves vulnerable to the depredations of another group from the northwest, the Minquas, who migrated from the Susquehanna River Valley via the waterways—the Chesapeake Bay to the Elk River in Maryland and then overland to the Christina. The emergence of a new trade economy between Indians on the one hand and various European ethnic groups on the other forced the men of the Leni-Lenape to concentrate their efforts on securing beaver pelts to the exclusion of other kinds of subsistence activities. Within a few decades the beaver, hunted down with guns, had been obliterated, and the Leni-Lenape turned to trading corn, fish, and venison, staples that allowed Swedish colonists to experiment with tobacco culture. In this weakened state, the Indians fell prey to the colonists' designs on their land, and by the 1680s they had scattered. Some pushed west into the interior; others were reduced to being day laborers in the service of the Swedes, then the Dutch, and then the English.[3]

As a settlement of people with roots in Europe and Africa, the town of Christiana has a history stretching back almost four centuries, and a diligent antiquarian would not have to look too long or hard to find an assortment of famous and quasi-famous people to associate with it. But by the mid-twentieth century the residents themselves lacked a sense of collective identity shaped by history. And by that time, the town's character as a backwater had foreclosed much in the way of hope for better times. Christiana lacked the charm of nearby New Castle, whose cobbled streets and eighteenth-century brick townhouses have been featured even recently in publications with titles like *The Sophisticated Traveler*.[4] Christiana also lacked the spanking-new freshness of the tract housing developments that were beginning to blanket New Castle County. Situated midway between the commercial center of Wilmington and the college town of Newark, and fifty miles north of the state capital of Dover, the town was too small and too poor to attract anyone's attention. People drove *through* it, but not *to* it.

In fact, people did pass through it on their way to many well-known tourist destinations. If we had pointed our Ford station wagon and driven an hour and a half, depending on the direction we took we could find ourselves on the boardwalk of Atlantic City, in the Pennsylvania-Dutch country of Lancaster in Pennsylvania, along the inland waterways of the Eastern Shore of Maryland, or at Independence Hall in Philadelphia. As a family we preferred to head south, down Route 13, past the migrant laborers stooped in the fields, over rivers with the names of Mispillion and Murderkill, and past the House of Fudge and Stuckey's, to Rehoboth Beach. There for one week each July we rented a whole house for $100 and prayed that bad weather would not spoil what amounted to fully half of my father's annual vacation.

The village of Christiana was located on the Christina, a thin little river that begins as a series of streams in the northwestern part of the state and within a few miles widens as it picks up several creeks (White Clay, Red Clay, and Mill) before finding its way to Wilmington and emptying into the Delaware River. I use the word "widens" in a relative sense only, for today the river (like the river I knew in the 1950s) is a sorry trickle of a thing, its muddy-mocha color evoking slow-moving sludge rather than the vital waterway of the Early Republic. For good reason we called it a creek (old-timers said "crick") and not a river. Although its forty miles represents a considerable portion of the length of New Castle County, in fact its beginning and end are separated by only twenty miles, if only the state bird, the blue hen, could fly in a direct line from the headwater of the river to its delta in the Delaware. Its modest physical dimensions and appearance notwithstanding, the Christina serves as a useful metaphor linking past to present, the way it once linked the Delaware tidewater region to the Maryland and Kentucky frontier.

Named for Queen Christina of Sweden by her explorer-subjects in the seventeenth century, the river has inspired some amount of poetic rhapsody. In 1654, an engineer for New Sweden (now Wilmington), described the Christina as a "deep river, rich in fish . . . yes [it is] such a fertile country that the pen is too weak to describe, praise and extol it, on account of its fertility it may well be called a land flowing with milk and honey."[5] Mary Vining, a belle of Wilmington during the Revolutionary era, flirted with a group of Patriot officers when she invoked the Christina: "That lovely stream moving languidly among its green banks always reminds me of a beautiful coquette, now coming here, now turning there, in playful waywardness."[6] A bard of the state, George Alfred Townsend, author of *Tales of the Chesapeake,* wrote of the beauty of New Castle County's "Netherlands scenery," and of the river's "full-bosomed tide raising and falling above the beautiful contour of its landscape . . . fading away into the level orchards, marshes and waters, the tinted hedgerows, cattle and sails."[7] An historian who sought to recover the history of the river in the late 1940s expressed appreciation for the way it "becomes relaxed and sinewless, meandering through a low-land of oak, sorghum, tulip, ash, and chestnut."[8]

In the colonial and early national period, Christiana Bridge (that was the town's original name) was a site of considerable strategic military significance. Beginning in the early seventeenth century, the surrounding area became a source of contention for a succession of colorful agents of empire, including the 400-pound John Printz of Sweden, whom the Indians called "Big Belly," and his compatriot, the silver-peg-legged Peter Stuyvesant. Christiana Bridge dates its re-corded history to 1679, when prominent landowners in the vicinity received an order from the colony of Pennsylvania to build a bridge over the Christina River. About this time the Calverts of Maryland and William Penn of Pennsylvania began to fight over who owned the place. George Talbot of Maryland (a cousin of Lord Baltimore) went so far as to erect a rude little fort to the west of present-day Christiana, and eight decades passed before his descendants gave up their claim. In 1704, the area wedged between the Delaware Bay and Maryland's eastern boundary outgrew its status as a stepchild of Pennsylvania—since 1682 William Penn had claimed for his own commonwealth the "Counties of New Castle, Kent, and Sussex on the Delaware"—and became a full-fledged colony in its own right. Two centuries ago, Christiana was worth defending with powder and shot.

The settlement owed its future prominence not only to the fact that it sat upon the banks of the Christina River, but also because it formed the crossroads between the highway running from Wilmington and Philadelphia (to the north) and the road linking New Castle (to the east) with Elkton and Baltimore (to the southwest). Christiana Bridge marked the upper reaches of the tidewater riverways that defined the Delaware coastal plain, and it served as the port for overland routes into the interior. Nevertheless, as a means of conveyance, the Christina lacked the glamour and ultimately the place in history that would distinguish its counterpart a few miles to the north, the Brandywine, which was swift enough to sustain any number of flour, textile, paper, and gun powder mills, the emblems and substance of a dynamic Delaware Valley.

Christiana Bridge early possessed a patriotic cast. In 1748 colonial officials removed official court records from New Castle to Christiana so they would not be confiscated or burned by the French and Spanish privateers plying Delaware Bay. Colonel John Read, the father of George, who signed the Declaration of Independence and was later a United States senator and the first chief justice of the Delaware Supreme Court, resided in the town; he lies buried in the cemetery of the Presbyterian Church. The two impressive, venerable brick structures that still stand at what is called "the Corner," the Christiana Inn and the Shannon Hotel, entertained a number of early-American notables. In the early 1760s, Mason and Dixon used Christiana Bridge as their base of operations when they located the point where the colonies of Maryland, Delaware, and Pennsylvania all came together, and then surveyed a line due west from that point, stretching almost three hundred miles into the Ohio Valley. That east-west line formed the boundary between Pennsylvania and Maryland, while a north-south extension separated Maryland from Delaware. During the Revolutionary War, both George Washington and the Marquis de Lafayette made brief appearances at Christiana Bridge while deploying American troops there. Their armies received supplies shipped up from Wilmington on boats called gondolas. In March 1781, fifteen hundred soldiers, under the command of Lafayette, started out from Christiana and advanced to Virginia, where they did battle with Benedict Arnold.

Today it requires an effort of the imagination to comprehend that the little stream known as Christina River served as a staging ground for men armed with field pieces, howitzers and cannon, as well as shot shells, powder, and other implements of war. In the 1950s, on my way home from school each day, I passed a tall steel blue and yellow historical marker that commemorated Lafayette's brief stopover in the town, but I remained skeptical of the claim that we had once played host to so much commotion. It is true, though, that this glorious moment in the town's history was encapsulated in the often-heard observation that George Washington had slept in both the liquor store and the sub shop, for those were the respective latter-day incarnations of the Christiana Inn and the Shannon Hotel.

By the time of the Revolution, the town had evolved from trade route to commercial hub. Low-draft sloops brought goods and staples upstream from Stanton, a milling center that processed wheat, lumber, cotton and snuff, and from Wilmington, now a major flour distribution center for the Delaware Valley. Lists of property owned by two Christiana Bridge Tories forced to flee to Pennsylvania during the war provide some idea of the prosperity of the area in the late eighteenth century. Included in the estates of James Dawson and James Wilson were evidence of a thriving agricultural economy (wheelbarrow rakes, haystacks, and fields of potatoes, pumpkins and beans, plus gardens "full of Sundry's"); a milling and manufacturing center (grindstones and looms for cotton, linen and wool production); and commerce (blankets, linens, and barrels of beef, pork, and flour, plus "Hogsheads of Spirituous Liquours & sundry other Moveables," deerskins, indigo, in addition to horses, light wagons, sloops, oar boats, and even a frigate).[9]

The town also witnessed several large and notable gatherings during the eighteenth century. The revivalist George Whitefield addressed "thousands" there in 1738; several hundred New Castle County Federalists met there in 1792 to protest recent taxes levied on steamboat operators and merchants to pay for a new college to be located in Newark; and a large crowd burned Supreme Court Chief Justice John Jay in effigy to denounce a recent treaty he had negotiated with Great Britain in 1795. These gatherings were all the more remarkable considering that, by the 1950s, it was rare to find more than a handful of Christiana residents in one place at one time—perhaps Sunday morning in one of the four churches, a Saturday night firehouse fund-raising supper, or a PTA meeting at the local school.

The river, prized too for its fish and waterfowl, and for the deer, muskrats, and squirrels that lived in the thickets covering its banks, was a lively place, a source of sustenance as well as a means of transportation. It was, indeed, an artery supplying blood to the heart of an early, enterprising America. By virtue of massive shipments of iron, flour, and flaxseed, the river became a commercial "highway" linking southern New Castle County with southern Pennsylvania and western Maryland.[10] In 1808 a visitor could observe Christiana's wharves piled high with as many as 20,000 flour barrels in the course of a single year. They were shipped up the river by boat, soon to be loaded onto wagons bound for Elkton, at the head of the Elk River, and then to points west. Four years later the wooden bridge that spanned the Christina was replaced by a stone one to better accommodate the six-team Conestoga wagons carrying goods overland to Maryland.

During the first decades of the nineteenth century, the town seemed to have a bright future. In 1813 the Elk and Christiana Turnpike Company invested in improvements to Old Baltimore Pike, the road between Wilmington and Baltimore. Nevertheless, storm clouds loomed on the horizon. The War of 1812 had already dealt a severe blow to the river's trade, and the town of Christiana Bridge began a precipitous decline. In the 1830s, nearby New Castle was chosen as the terminus for the New Castle-Frenchtown steam railroad connecting the Delaware River to the Elk River. And to the south, also on the banks of the Delaware River, Delaware City was beginning to thrive, thanks to a new canal cutting through from the Delaware to the Chesapeake Bay. Christiana even suffered from the 1825 opening of the Erie Canal, which became the major trade route between the East Coast and the Great Lakes.

As early as 1840, then, some might say that the town's best days lay behind it, now that people and goods loaded on trains and canal boats had begun to pass it by. Peters General Store, located near the center of town, continued to serve residents until the late nineteenth century, but its customers were small farmers, not merchants. Meanwhile, New Castle County landowners were draining the swamps that bordered the Christina. Deprived of its many small sources, the river slowly shriveled, dried up, and disappeared from the economic life of the region. Around that time, travellers en route from Newark to New Castle might pass through Christiana, "its commerce gone and glory departed," in the words of one local historian, and pause on the bridge, over "the sluggish stream that in years back had had an important history of which [people now] knew little and cared less. . . ."[11]

In 1950 the town consisted of about seventy-five houses, the same number that had existed on the site in 1770, and only a handful of enduring family names connected the halcyon 1790s with the moribund mid-twentieth century. When I was growing up, no living person could have remembered the glory days built on barrels of grain.

Of the history of the fifty or sixty African Americans who inhabited Christiana in the 1950s we have little specific information. The configuration of their small neighborhood provides some clues. The children I came to know at school spoke with Delaware accents. They were probably not recent migrants to the state, but rather the great-great-grandchildren of slaves who had been freed in New Castle County during the early nineteenth century. The history of bondage in Delaware conformed to the state's larger bifurcated nature. Downstate the most prosperous farmers of Sussex County fancied themselves great planters in the southern style, and in the early nineteenth century one of their neighbors, Patty Cannon, achieved legendary status as both a kidnapper of free blacks, who were then spirited away to southern slaveholders, and as a murderer of cash-laden slave traders. In contrast, in the northern part of the state, commerce demanded little in the way of bound labor, and Thomas Garrett, a Wilmington Quaker, likewise secured for himself a place in Delaware history textbooks for his work with Harriet Tubman in keeping the Underground Railroad open to hundreds of southern slaves who survived the treacherous journey to freedom.

Two decades before the Civil War, slavery was a weakened institution in Delaware. Out of a white population of 58,000 people, only 900 owned 3,300 slaves, and these were concentrated in the two lower counties of Kent and Sussex. The 16,000 free people of color constituted fully 20 percent of the state's population, but this beleaguered group suffered from what one contemporary called whites' "FEAR of the free colored people pervading the community."[12] Emulating the restrictive policies applied to free blacks imposed by states to the south, and foreshadowing the constraints under which freedpeople would live after the war, antebellum Delaware placed restrictions on free blacks' ability to own firearms, gather for religious worship, or preach. Blacks were not allowed to testify against whites in trials, nor were they permitted to serve on juries or vote or hold office. Failure to abide by these (and criminal) laws could result in the sale of the offender to the highest bidder, as part of a system of involuntary servitude. In 1841, the state convicted a black man, Moses McColly, for "cuting a sapling" and fined him five dollars. Because he was unable to pay the fine and court costs, Mc-

Colly was "sold to the highest bidder in or out of the state for 7 years." Notwithstanding the existence of upstanding farmers, mechanics, and builders among the free black population, the vast majority were laborers and servants. Dominated by Democrats after the Civil War, Delaware stubbornly retained discriminatory policies characteristic of the former Confederate states.

By the mid-twentieth century, black families in Christiana were clustered on a back street called Brown's Lane and a tiny spur off it, Neury's Lane. They possessed no large landholdings, but rather kept chickens and tended vegetable gardens to supplement whatever wages they earned—in the case of black men, probably as seasonal laborers; of black women, probably as domestics and laundresses. In this general region were located Delaware 111-C (for "colored") public elementary school, built by the philanthropist Pierre S. DuPont and dedicated in 1920; and two small black churches, close by each other— Mount Pleasant African Methodist Episcopal Zion (founded in 1880) and the other, Old Fort Union African Methodist Episcopal Church, probably founded around the same time. Though both were offshoots of the Methodist Church in Delaware, whose origins stretched back to 1784, these two African American congregations were allied with distinct denominations. Mount Pleasant was founded by a former Kent County slave, Richard Allen, in Philadelphia in the early 1790s; Old Fort Union was started by Peter Spencer in Wilmington in 1813. The existence of the two church buildings and the school suggests that a cohesive African American community existed in Christiana by the post-Civil War period, although it was small and largely impoverished.

In the 1950s, from the perspective of outsiders, Christiana amounted to little more than a tiny settlement located at "the Corner," where Delaware Route 7 (divided into East Main Street and West Main Street) came together with North and South Old Baltimore Pike. Each of two short byways served as a hypotenuse of sorts, with Water-McGuire Street, only a few hundred yards long, connecting East Main Street to the south spur of Old Baltimore Pike, and Brown's Lane linking the north part of the Pike to West Main Street.

The Corner itself consisted of four notable buildings. Baldwin's Market was a jumble of a general store in front of a dwelling owned by the proprietor. Built in the early twentieth century and covered with tarpaper shingles, it was a two-story structure with a sagging front porch and a world-weary air about it. Kitty-cornered was the Christiana Fire House, a sprawling white stucco building holding fire trucks of increasing variety and sophistication as the years went by. The Fire Company itself was an active and prosperous fraternal order, complete with Women's Auxiliary and enriched by seemingly endless fund raisers in the form of dances, raffles, and turkey dinners. Periodically the air was rent with the wail of the fire siren, which went off with alarming frequency around the clock. As the firefighters invested in new equipment, they extended their reach into the surrounding areas of New Castle County.

Directly across from the firehouse was the historic Christiana Hotel (in the 1950s the Christiana Package Store) and across from Baldwin's was the Shannon Inn that I knew as the Sub Shop, a large whitewashed brick house with a distinctive Mid-Atlantic pent roof adorning half of the front. Cobbled onto the right side of the Sub Shop was a two-story structure, little more than lean-to. Next to it was a stucco-covered brick two-family residence, formerly Odd Fellows Hall, and before that Peters General Store.

If you stood at the Corner, you could walk to all of the town's major institutions within a matter of minutes—to the north, the Presbyterian Church, founded in 1732, an imposing white stucco building dating back to 1857; and not far beyond it, on the same side of the street, the two black churches, one brick and one frame. A little further on stood an abandoned wooden building, formerly 111-C, the public school for black children. To the west of the Corner was the white Methodist Church founded in 1857; and then up the street on the same side, Delaware School 44 for white children, both substantial brick buildings.

I should state here that the town was devoid of the character that might have derived from some interesting and pleasing topographical features. It could boast no vistas across wide bodies of water, broad fields, or hills, and in the winter it was marked by an almost unspeakable bleakness owing to the predominance of deciduous trees. The Christina was too brown and shriveled to call forth the praise that had been lavished on it to centuries earlier. Beginning in 1957, with the opening of the Getty Oil Refinery a few miles south in Delaware City, rainstorms brought the stench of crude oil to the town. Still, it offered a place to live that was quieter and cheaper than both Wilmington and Newark. After World War II, major industries fanned out into the suburbs of New Castle County, and Christiana at-

tracted southern migrants, especially from Tennessee, who sought
good-paying union jobs at the nearby Chrysler and General Motors
auto assembly plants.

The town's eclectic history was inscribed in its diverse architecture,
much underappreciated by all concerned in the 1950s. In addition to
the fine examples of colonial homes of either stucco or brick, were
narrow, wooden houses in the nineteenth-century Mid-Atlantic farmhouse style, and a few modest early twentieth-century bungalows. The
plain brick, two-story Methodist Church imitated the general style of
its Mother Church, Barratt's Chapel ("the cradle of American Meth-
odism"), in Kent County. The stately Presbyterian Church, rendered
in the style of a medieval chapel and perched on an embankment
above North Old Baltimore Pike, remained the most impressive
structure in town. A federal Works Progress Administration crew constructed the gray stone bridge that spanned the river. Walking along
East Main Street as it sloped down from the Corner to the river and
then on to my parents' house would take no more than ten minutes
or so. Along the way one would encounter the brown stucco and
wooden clapboard houses of auto workers newly arrived from the
South, the Webber and Lewden houses constructed during the eighteenth century, a colonial-style brick house built by a now deceased
physician in the 1930s, and next to that, my grandfather's house, a
graceful two-story, New England white wood-frame colonial.

My grandparents had picked their house out of a Sears Roebuck
catalog in 1932. (Representing a variety of styles and sizes, a few other
Sears houses went up in Delaware in the 1920s and 1930s.) The
pieces of the prefabricated dwelling had been delivered to Stanton
on flatbed railroad cars, and trucked to Christiana. Then a couple of
carpenters, under my grandfather's direction, proceeded to assem-
ble it. In effect, my grandparents had managed to use that conve-
nient consumer device, the mail-order catalog, to recreate a bit of
their Yankee heritage in Christiana. An unreconstructed hater of
President Franklin Roosevelt and the New Deal he created, my grandfather liked to claim that he had sponsored his own private version of
a public works project by employing these house carpenters in the
depths of the Depression.

Feeding into the town's institutions were the residents of the surrounding countryside and two other, even smaller hamlets—Bear to
the south and Salem to the west. In this constricted world, all settlements were relative. Thus, a family moving from Smalley's Mill Road

(a couple of miles outside of Christiana), into the old Odd Fellows Building, could view the experience as akin to moving from a rural area into "town." For them, the Corner afforded a more lively everyday scene, with periodic traffic accidents at the crossroads, the coming and going of fire trucks across the street, and the general consternation caused by the occasional flooding of the Christina River a couple of blocks away.

Still, the fact remains that we had no town government and no town services, and it was a sign of Christiana's dejected condition that there existed no commercial establishment where one might sit down to eat or drink, let alone sleep or watch a movie. Leadership splintered among the four churches, the public schools, and the fire company. A small group calling itself the Christiana Improvement Association kept alive the flame of civic engagement. In June of 1956 for example they sponsored a card party at the firehouse and used the proceeds to benefit the streetlight fund, but their meetings were irregular and sparsely attended. While the Corner gave the place a physical center, the town lacked a public, or political, center.

Despite its size, Christiana was remarkably diverse. People who lived there could be classified by all manner of social signifiers usually interpreted as social differences. Whites divided between the Methodists and Presbyterians; blacks between the UAME and the AME members. There were old-timers and newcomers; wage earners and salaried professionals; progressives who fought to consolidate the town with the Newark public school district and the conservatives who fought against consolidation; Republicans and Democrats; Delaware natives and those who still identified with the regional and class culture they had left behind, either hardscrabble Appalachia or rock-ribbed New England; young hoods and old geezers; those who walked to school and those who were bused to school from the surrounding countryside.

Over the course of the decade I came to understand another, subterranean fissure dividing the town—the one between boys and girls, men and women. This last division remained submerged most of the time, revealed to me only infrequently, when my friend Mary Ann Fitzgerald whispered that her uncle wanted to "put his train in her tunnel," when I heard rumors of "bad girls" packed off to Baltimore to have their babies in secret and in shame, and when I learned that the mother of one of my friends had taken her youngest child (and him alone) and left a husband who had beaten her.

The town's small population afforded a surprisingly large number of males of various ages whom I mostly admired from afar, including the teenagers—Stevie Berger, the older brother of my two-doors-down neighbor Joanie; Jimmy Harvey and Chip Weatherby, the good-looking hoods; Alan Comer, our church organist who could play anything at all without written music; and my contemporaries, Les Harper with his flattop, Marty Cobb with his ducktail. At various times during the 1950s, the mere sight of any one of them made my life worth living.

Just under the surface of this tired old place then pulsed the uneven but passionate rhythms of an odd little society.

My own family's sense of place, theoretically shaped by a distinctive mid-Atlantic history and culture, was decidedly muted. The Sunday-afternoon sounds of guests using shell crackers to work their way through the bushels of hardshell crabs my uncle had imported from the Chesapeake; the smell of scrapple (a spicy, heavily larded pork sausage) frying in our kitchen on a Saturday morning; the sight of the Canadian geese who made a temporary home for themselves in the pond behind our house, a stop on the north-south flyway—these memories gain meaning only in hindsight, for we were oblivious to their larger significance at the time.

My grandparents' house lay close by the Christina, and the tangle of underbrush, poison sumac, and honeysuckle that rimmed the backyard yielded a certain unkempt lushness, at least in the summer. In 1951, six years after they were married and three years after I was born, my parents built their modest white stucco house at the end of East Main Street. We were surrounded on two sides (across the road and to the right) by woods. To the left stood my grandparents' house and in the back of our house was a pond.

From an early age I was conscious of the fact that the icons of homelife as revealed on 1950s TV yielded no clues to our literal or figurative place in postwar America. Unlike the characters on shows like *Leave it to Beaver,* or *Father Knows Best,* we had no sidewalk in front of our house, but neither did we live on a farm, like the family in *Lassie.* The apartments inhabited by Lucy and Ricky Ricardo and Alice and Ralph Cramden represented a strange and remote world. Perhaps it was a failure of the language, for no term adequately conveyed our setting. "Village" sounded too New England-y, "town" too substantial, "settlement" too frontier-like. On an urban-suburban-rural continuum, we remained in limbo.

By the time any motorists arrived at the Corner and sat for forty seconds waiting for the red light to change, they were in the mood to hurry up and get to wherever they were going, and so accelerated on the stretch of road in front of our house. Each of the dogs we owned in succession—a part-German shepherd, part-collie was the perennial mutt of choice—developed the bad habit of chasing cars. As a result, we grew accustomed to a continuous, predictable litany of noises outside our front door: the sound of a speeding car and then the squealing of tires and the jamming of brakes, followed by a yelping dog and often a cursing driver. My father did not like to tie up a dog with a rope or chain in the backyard, so we doted on a series of dogs which we were loathe to restrain. We loved our dogs for as long as they lived. We showed the same serial affection to our cats, often the offspring of my grandmother's fat cat Gus; but these animals too inevitably met with an untimely end, crushed under the tires of a passing car, or even of our own car, heading out the driveway; plucked from the backyard by an owl; bloodied by a stray dog. The cycle of pets seemed to us to be in the natural order of things.

Using the dirt lane that ran parallel to East Main Street and connected our place to my grandmother's next door, I roamed back and forth between the two houses several times a day and never bothered to knock before slipping into her kitchen through the back door. If I saw no one downstairs I went upstairs, where I might find my grandmother sewing or my aunt reading. Neither one ever seemed startled to see me.

By 1956 we were a family of four. The house we lived in consisted of the basics—downstairs the living room, dining room, and kitchen, upstairs three bedrooms—the plastered walls all painted in pastels called warm peach and robin's egg blue. The furnishings showed my mother's handiwork as an upholsterer and seamstress. We lived in a domestic garden of floral prints, surrounded by an array of colorful flowers in the curtains and bedspreads, and on the sofa, the chairs, and the dishtowels hanging from the oven door.

One of my brothers was born in 1953 and the other three years later. For the most part, I regarded both of them with a mixture of indifference and aloofness. The older one appeared to me in several different guises, depending upon what he had received for his birthday or Christmas that year—as a railroad engineer in black and white striped denim overalls with matching cap; a cowboy outfitted with guns and shod in red and white boots, with matching hat; a baseball player in a full jersey, with, yes, a matching cap. He would also surface in my consciousness every once in a while playing other scripted parts—at age four, for example, he was dutiful pupil learning to read and write under my imperious tutelage. My other brother brilliantly assumed the role of the spoiled baby, and he had some intriguing qualities. He could amuse himself for hours on end with tiny Matchbox cars and trucks, and if he did not get his way he would let out a high, piercing scream that prompted everyone else to let him have his way, and quickly. I well remember that scream, its pitch and timbre, because it was the loudest human noise I heard at home while growing up.

In the stucco house on East Main Street, the emotional affect, the expression of family feeling, was as flat as a downstate beanfield. In this regard the books, magazines and newspapers that littered the downstairs—piled up in the living room, spilling over the kitchen counter, scattered on the dining room floor—testified less to our messy house (though that was also the case) and more to the primacy of reading material over verbal engagement. We did not often all share the living room at the same time. My father and mother were busy with meetings at school and at church, but by the late 1950s whatever everyday "family time" we had, we spent together all reading pieces of the newspaper to ourselves, not out loud. Many years later the spouses who married into the family would declare this hushed, collective ritual of absorption in the daily paper to be the distinguishing feature of the Joneses. Indeed, a hallmark of family life was our ability to sit in the same room together for long periods of time without talking to each other. Relative to other families that I would become acquainted with in the coming years, ours failed to foster much in the way of a verbal culture.

My mother set the tone for the family, and it was a decidedly subdued one. When I was growing up, I never once heard her swear or raise her voice in rage, in criticism of one of us or anyone else, in desperation or exasperation. Having known her for fifty years now, I can still say the same; I do know, however, that three-quarters of a century after the fact, she still feels awful about throwing the mustard jar at her sister. Still it was a measure of my mother's nature that her visible idiosyncracies were so few and so meager. At the time, I marveled only that she did not sleep with a pillow at night, and that she did not like the salt-and-sugar taste of peanut butter and jelly sandwiches, nor did she like raspberries. Otherwise she seemed to have no quirks, no bad habits. In the universal pantheon of eccentric family members, she would forever remain conspicuous for her absence.

If my mother was extraordinary in her even temperament, my father was more ordinary in the sense that he had a temper that he struggled to control. More than once in a while he would tremble with anger, on the verge of eruption, and my mother would leap into action, tamping him down with a few well-chosen words of reassurance, words intended to warn as well as calm him. Restraint was a secular religion of sorts: Thou shalt not shout.

Quiet did not always signal acquiescence. I remember one muggy, mid-summer Sunday afternoon, the kind of Delaware day that swaths you in a hot, wet, wool blanket. After dinner, my brothers ran outside and I went upstairs to my room while my parents stayed at the dining room table. Starting back down the stairs, I overheard my father trying to contain his rage. His voice was low, modulated, barely under control. I froze on the top step.

"Don't you EVER again insist that I wear a jacket and tie to church on a day like this," he said to my mother.

I ran through my head the conversation that must have transpired that morning, as they were getting dressed for church.

My mother made a plea for appropriate Sunday attire while my father expressed some apprehension over sitting through a steam-bath of a service. My mother won the battle that morning but she lost the wider war that afternoon. Thereafter my father would attend church wearing a tieless white shirt whenever he wanted. Though relatively innocuous, this exchange remained part of my memory because it was so unusual, and so unusually revealing of our toned-down family.

The quiet that characterized the household also derived from the fact that we had few personal or family crises to contend with. The flow of our lives proceeded through narrow channels shaped by daily and seasonal routines, the waters unroiled by either internal conflicts or external tragedies. We suffered from no debilitating diseases, and even emergency trips to the doctor were limited in number: one brother received the family's only stitches (to close a wound when he fell into the corner of the living room coffee table), and my mother suffered the family's only broken bone when she fell in the snow on the way to the post office one day. Together, we buttressed our good luck with a great deal of caution.

More tellingly, our encounters with representatives of the judicial and legal systems were few in number. I do not recall any lawyer ever entering our home. We heard the fire siren and watched the fire trucks roar by every day but the firefighters themselves we met face-to-face only once, when my brother and a friend were playing with matches and accidentally set fire to a field near our house. The county police made appearances infrequently—one time, when the reddest in our series of Ford station wagons was stolen out of our driveway in broad daylight, later to be recovered, full of purloined watches, in Florida; and the other times when late-night drivers fell asleep at the wheel or succumbed to drink and, missing the turn at the end of Hare's Corner Road, came crashing into my father's garden. The ensuing confusion—police cars, the ambulance to haul the body to the hospital or the corpse to the morgue, the gaggle of curious passersby—constituted an unfortunate and all-too-often occurrence, but one that disturbed our sleep one night at a time, and not our lives.

If any sinister force menaced us it was the Delaware Highway Department, in our minds a state agency populated by bureaucrats who would not rest as long as a shred of greenery remained in New Castle County. As a youngster I was only vaguely aware of its ugly motives, but I did understand that my father periodically battled the department and its minions, appearing before zoning commission boards and appealing decisions that threatened to destroy the snug little world we had made for ourselves. As a crossroads set smack in the middle of New Castle County, Christiana was too tempting for overzealous highway planners to resist for long. My father won some and he lost some of his fights with the department, probably relishing the contest for its own sake. In any case the road in front of our house widened perceptibly over the years. Still, he managed to contain his frustration and save his heated words for the county commissioners, far out of our earshot.

In fact, my father relished local politics of all kinds—he was active in the church and served on the Christiana school board from 1956 to 1960—but at home he retreated, for at least four months of the year, to his beloved vegetable garden. There he could labor in peace, without worrying that the green peppers or tomatoes would give him a hard time about anything. Inside the house, he had few defining passions. He was a great fan of the writers Mickey Spillane and James Michener, but he cared little about either professional sports or domestic household matters broadly defined.

My father was a chain-smoker. As a result, all of us moved around the house enveloped in a blue-gray haze, day in and day out. I early became fascinated by the intricate rituals he followed to light up and take a drag on a "fag," as he called it. Holding a silky smooth, shiny aluminum cigarette lighter in one hand, he would flick it once, twice, and then lean into it, until the end of his Marlboro glowed orange-red. Then he would tilt his head back and blow the smoke up and outwards. He could talk, Bogart-like, with a cigarette hanging out of his mouth, and in fact, he could do most anything while he was smoking—read, watch TV, eat dinner, talk on the telephone, pay the bills. The living room was littered with ashtrays of various sizes and shapes, filled to overflowing with butts, ashes, and the red and white cellophane packages of his favorite (and only) brand. At the store, he and my mother purchased cigarettes by the carton, never by the pack. Today I marvel that he lived to be seventy-six years old.

My father's modest ascent up the DuPont corporate ladder would end abruptly on a rung that defined us as solidly middle class but by no stretch of the imagination upper-middle class. Without a college degree he remained stymied, and over the years endured a series of bosses, each one younger than the one before. At the same time, he negotiated an informal contract with DuPont; in return for his ever-greater public profile the company would allow him to spend time away from work on school business. He won election to the Newark Board in 1964, serving until 1974, when he was appointed by Governor Sherman Tribbitt as president of the State Board of Education, a post he held at the pleasure of the three successive governors (Pete Du Pont and Michael Castle after Tribbitt), until 1986. DuPont corporate public-relations considerations thus allowed my father to escape the fate of the classic "organization man."[13]

At home, I overheard a great deal about my father's politicking, but within the household, the constricted boundaries of acceptable behavior decreed that there should be no overt displays of displeasure or unhappiness. More profoundly, moodiness of any kind was not tolerated: *Wipe that pout off your face* was my parents' admonition. We were not allowed the luxury of revealing our deepest resentments, and we chafed under the enforced cheerfulness that at times seemed more oppressive than any honestly expressed anger could ever be.

The superficial serenity of our everyday lives might have been less remarkable had we all stayed awake all night, prowling around the house and venting our anxieties. Yet here again, peace and quiet prevailed, for family culture dictated that, after the lights were extinguished at a reasonable hour, no one should venture downstairs until he or she was ready to eat breakfast. As far as I knew, we were a family of sound sleepers. It is true that I had no familiarity with insomnia, either the word or the concept, until I was much older. My mother and father could each partake of a cup of black coffee at eleven at night while they watched the evening news, and afterwards go to bed and fall asleep immediately. Only on TV sitcoms did I learn of such a thing as a midnight raid on the refrigerator; the notion of consuming food while others slept was foreign to me. This is not to say that I slept through every night. I had no compunction about waking my mother when my stomach hurt, or a nightmare struck, or when the sticky heat of a July night left me soaked with sweat, tossing and turning. But these were instances of discomfort, notable for their infrequency, and when I went to rouse my mother, I invariably found that she and my father (and my brothers for that matter) were asleep.

We reveled in our own normality, and in the way we glossed over conflict and frustration: as a household, ours had all the characteristics of a neurosis-free zone.

If I had to choose a single principle that defined the way we thought about ourselves, it would be: if you could plug it in, we wanted it. My mother secretly hailed the first electric vacuum cleaner we owned. Her old-fashioned father had always resisted buying household machines of all kinds because he considered them a waste of money. Similarly, she was happy to leave behind the treadle sewing machine that she had grown up with and, as a bride, graduate to a fancy electric one. With a family discount at my uncle's General Electric appliance store in Newport, we managed to boast both a clothes dryer and a dishwasher in Christiana relatively early in the mid-1950s. We slept under electric blankets and ate roasts carved by an electric knife. To dry my hair I wore a gigantic, bouffant hood attached to a hot-air blower by a plastic tube. Waffle iron, blender, electric frying pan, toaster, electric coffeepot and clock radio stood ready in the kitchen, but we passed up the electric can opener and the electric pencil sharpener simply because after a while there was no place to plug them in. We switched on a television (as of 1953) in the living room, hi-fi in the dining room, dehumidifier and commercial-size freezer in the basement, electric fans in the kids' bedrooms, and an air conditioner in the parents' bedroom. It was therefore understandable when one of my uncles received an electric fork one Christmas—a large fork with an electric cord and plug attached to it—it took me a while to figure out that it was a gag gift. The most significant document detailing our vigorous middle-class status was our monthly electric bill.

We kept up public appearances, as all Joneses were supposed to do, with a new Ford station wagon every three or four years. The car was our crowning glory, for it represented who we were for all the world to see. More the pity, then, that my father drove it to work almost every day, leaving my mother to fend for herself with an old thing that had belonged to my grandfather—a hideous, late-forties Ford sedan. Purple and bloated, it reminded me of the blood-swollen ticks that fell off our dog and onto the living-room rug or kitchen linoleum. Its woolen seat covers were an endless source of torment to me and my brothers as we waited in the car for what seemed to be an eternity while our mother did her errands. This car was old and round, not new and sleek, its color dull and dark, not bright and shiny like the new models. I couldn't stand the sight or the musty smell of it.

As a family, we early on established brand loyalties that gradually became sacrosanct. Our appliances were made by General Electric, not Westinghouse or Sears. Since my mother sewed most of what she and I wore, I was unaware of clothing brands; we shopped at Sears and J.C. Penney for shoes and underwear. I divided the world into a series of dyads: We drove a Ford, not (the foreign-sounding) Chevrolet; we pumped Sunoco, not Flying A; we used Crest, not Pepsodent; my father worked for DuPont, not General Motors; we preferred Perry Como over Bing Crosby; we were Presbyterians and Republicans, not Methodists and Democrats.

Juxtaposed to the material bounty we took for granted, however, were certain retrograde aspects of our household that served as a constant reminder we were not yet fully within the mainstream of consumer culture. Since Christiana was not incorporated, it provided no town utilities. Our septic system piped sewage into the backyard where, after a heavy rain, foul-smelling stuff percolated up through the ground. We burned our own trash in a rusty oil drum in the woods behind the house, where rats made their homes in the discarded bottles and cans, and bits of burning newspaper floating skyward threatened to ignite the trees nearby. We pumped our own water out of a well, its rusty color staining everything it touched—the bathtub and sinks, clothes, dishes, linens, teeth.

I spent a great deal of time exploring the compact little world around our house. Whatever the time of year and whatever the weather, in the daylight hours I was more likely to be outside the house than inside. Weekdays were consumed by school and homework for me and my brothers and by work or housework and nighttime meetings for our parents, and Sundays given over to church and visits with extended family members; Saturday was a day of potential togetherness. Instead, I usually started the day at my grandmother's house, where I would have the opportunity to spend time with my unmarried aunt. She worked as a secretary for a DuPont Company executive, but her job title gave little indication of her responsibilities. Moreover, corporate policies allowed her to advance no further regardless of her considerable intelligence and formal education, a B.A. in history from the University of Delaware.

A close examination of contemporary family photos reveals her essential primness—wireless glasses, short hair neatly marcelled. At the time, she struck me as undeniably gorgeous, a fifties career girl (albeit one whose time outside of work was consumed by caring for her elderly mother and serving as a pillar of the church). In her bedroom she had a vanity table crowded with little glass bottles of sweet-smelling things, and no matter how early I arrived in the morning her bed was made, and the rest of the room immaculate, a stark contrast to the disorderly house I lived in.

Downstairs while she sat at the dull-brown piano and practiced the hymns we would sing at Sunday School the next day, I would poke around my grandfather's office (right off the living room), where his surveyors' tools hung on the walls above his desk, even years after his death. Or I might climb onto the sofa and page through the latest issue of the *Saturday Evening Post,* waiting patiently for her to finish playing so that we could do errands in her car. She bought a new car every couple of years, and rather incongruously, it was always a huge thing, a flashy Buick, Oldsmobile, or Pontiac sprouting the biggest fins, the longest and widest wings, that money could buy. Later, when we drove up the long dusty lane to the Wilsons' farm to buy eggs, we arrived in style.

Back at my grandmother's, I might venture out to the deserted chicken coop in the backyard, sidestepping the poison ivy and tiptoeing through the shards of broken glass that littered the inside and outside of the crumbling structure, ever vigilant to the black snakes that sought shelter in it. Or I might head off to the garage built for the trucks and other equipment used in my grandfather's business. Six bays long, it was now used to store some of the belongings of our minister who had recently returned from missionary work in Korea. There, next to the work benches supporting vises and axe sharpeners, I found delicate, tasseled fans, beaded necklaces, and fragile porcelain bowls with pictures of green dragons. In 1955, when I was seven, the minister died, and in accordance with his last will and testament, the church auctioned off the possessions he had stored in my grandmother's garages and earned for itself the munificent and much needed sum of $2700.

On Saturday afternoon, or for that matter almost any day of the year when the weather was half-decent, I would go down the hill behind our house to the pond, a pristine little body of water that represented the moral center of my childhood. My grandfather, a civil engineer and surveyor, had made a comfortable living for his family of ten. In 1924 they had settled in Christiana, taking over the one-hundred-fifty-year-old Webber House that was constantly in danger of flooding from the river, which flowed within a couple hundred feet of the house. After a decade they moved to his new, Sears-made house just down the street and across the river. There my grandfather started a sand and gravel business, dredging from a natural spring and in the process creating a one-acre pond. Throughout the Great Depression, and through part of World War II, the pond was the site of much vigorous activity, the handiwork of my grandfather's self-taught know-how.

Floating in the pond's middle and mounted on barrels, a barge held the pumping machinery that extracted sand and gravel and ran these materials up through a steep pipe that poured them into four large wooden bins supported by cement walls. These bins were covered with varied-mesh screens used to separate everything into fine sand, coarse sand, pebbles and stones. Dump trucks, of two- to five-ton capacity, backed up under the appropriate bin, and a trap door released the bin's contents into the back of the trucks. My grandfather's sandpit-fed concrete mixers serviced construction sites throughout Wilmington, among other places. His logo read:

H. A. PHELPS
WASHED SAND AND GRAVEL

What this small business lacked in glamour it made up in solidity and predictability.

In 1944, my grandfather had sold his equipment to another sand-and-gravel operator not far away, and by the time I was born all that remained of the operation were the cement walls, now stripped of their bins. But what remained of the pond was more than enough for me, a gem of blues, greens, and yellows that sparkled in the summer sun. I believed its beauty was beyond describing. It was not a sandpit any more, because the steep banks were overgrown with bushes and trees, smothered in honeysuckle that rimmed the water with green in the spring and summer. Neither did it resemble a farm pond, for it was recessed into the woods, undetectable from the road that ran in front of our house. And it was not a quarry; the bottom was soft sand, though covered in places by underwater vegetation, and there were no rocks to make swimming dangerous.

During the summer my cousins and brothers and I spent many of our afternoons paddling around in the pond, diving for pebbles and chasing the sunfish. If we stood still for too long, hashing over the plot of some TV show we had seen the night before, the sunnies would nibble our legs; they found the moles on our arms, legs, and backs especially appealing. Some days we would stay on shore and try to retaliate, casting out homemade fishing lines baited with spitballs of bread, but we never knew what to do with what we caught, and nobody relished prying a slippery, smelly thing with sharp fins off a hook to begin with; so mostly we left the fish alone.

Exploring the pond from a rickety rowboat, we could search for garter snakes and, pushing the weeping willow branches out of the way, drift languidly into a tiny cove where the surface was covered with dancing waterbugs. We would whisper so that we did not scare the row of turtles sunning on a log. Or we might lie in the grass on "the point," a small spit of land that reached out into the water, watching dragonflies flit among the blueberry bushes or butterflies dance above the daisies. In all kinds of weather we constructed "forts" out of fallen branches in the woods, and conducted expeditions that took us the entire way around the pond, following a makeshift path up and down the banks (we called them hills), and over the shallow stream lined with skunk cabbage that emptied into the Christina River.

In the winter, when the water froze, as it did for a few weeks most every year, we dragged our Flexible Flyers up an embankment we called Monkey Hill, flopped down on them, closed our eyes, and pushed off, sliding down a forty-five-degree incline and taking the all-too-often bloody nose in stride. We would ice-skate by the light of a fading sun in the late afternoon, after school, and stop to peer at the frogs and air bubbles encased in the ice. On weekend nights we might build a fire on the point and skate by its light until bedtime.

Always drawn to personal melodrama, I loved to roam the hidden pathways around the pond by myself, looking for whatever I was collecting that day (acorns, feathers, smooth "skipping" stones) and torture myself with a scenario that seemed inevitable: My father comes home from work one evening, slowly removes his felt hat, and announces to the family that the DuPont Company is transferring him. We must move. I must leave this most perfect spot on earth. My life has just ended, and I am doomed to descend into the hell of a tract housing development. Don't they know that my soul, my very being, is lodged here in the sand of the spot where we swim, that not blood but pond water courses through my veins?

The pond was a personal space, because I fancied myself a loner in any case, but it was also a collective space, one that I shared with my cousins and brothers all the time, and with my aunts and uncles too on the Fourth of July. At the pond I learned my first lessons distinguishing private from public property. When teenage boys from the surrounding area ventured into the pond to swim or onto its banks to fish, they inevitably encountered my father, who, with hands on hips, recited the pronouncement that I must have heard hundreds of times: "This is private property. Trespassing is not allowed. If you do not leave I will have to call the police." They left.

The rude reception accorded these boys who dared to venture into our much envied little compound suggested that we lived in the town but at the same time felt a need to maintain a certain distance from it. In fact, our neighbors were never guests in our home. It is true that my parents drew upon the resources of the town for baby-sitting services, but the two kindly, elderly women who were our favorites never shared a meal with our family. Mrs. Wilder, a widow who had recently moved from Nashville, was a small woman with a face deeply etched with wrinkles, a sight made all the more striking by the fact that she had no teeth. (I reportedly told my mother one day, "I like Mrs. Wilder but she's almost worn out.")

Mrs. Tegelaar, a tall, painfully thin widow, her sparse hair secured firmly with a light-brown hairnet, inadvertently provided me with one of the most memorable evenings of my childhood when she announced that her son, Johnny, a chef who worked at the DuPont Country Club, would be stopping by our house to visit her later. Mrs. TG, as we called her, was a sweet, hopelessly old-fashioned soul living in a small house between Baldwin's store and the Presbyterian Church. Therefore I was startled when Johnny roared up our driveway on his immense motorcycle. Clad in a black leather jacket, his dark hair swept up in a pompadour, he was an Elvis clone. He kissed his sweet old mother while I stood nearby, trembling. I had never seen such a gorgeous, un-Phelps-like sight as Johnny Tegelaar.

My mother had attended elementary school with a number of the mothers and fathers of my friends, and she was always a reliable guide through the genealogical thicket of several entangled, extended families in the town. I had friends among all these families, though I was never certain who was a cousin of whom. Their fathers were electricians, body-shop workers, employees of Chrysler and General Motors, and firehouse volunteers. Many of them, especially those who lived right outside of town, kept chickens and goats and tended orchards and gardens. Most attended the Methodist Church.

Although my mother knew many of these families well and I saw their children daily, we did not socialize with them. On Easter, Thanksgiving or Christmas we might have relatives for dinner. For her part, my mother regularly met with a group of friends whom she had met in college at the University of Delaware. They rotated their monthly "Girls' Club" luncheon among the dozen or so "members," most of whom lived in the suburbs north of Wilmington. Some Saturday nights my parents would host another married couple, friends they saw at church or knew from my father's work. The four of them would sit at a card table set up in the living room and play canasta or bridge until midnight. The next morning I would find the remains of their evening—ashtrays filled with cigarette stubs, bowls with a few stale pretzels and salted peanuts, glasses with lipstick on the rim, crumpled cocktail napkins. With the exception of my aunt and grandmother who lived next door, all of our guests arrived by car; they lived that far away.

Visiting my friends, I marveled at the differences between their living quarters and my own. A couple years older than I, Joanie Berger lived right down the road from us in a substantial Georgian brick house between my grandfather's house and Christiana Bridge. Her father was a chemist who worked at the DuPont plant in Deepwater, New Jersey. The Bergers were virtually the only family in Christiana that could be labeled upper-middle class. Like many young girls, Joanie early developed a love of and obsession with horses, but unlike most, she was given a horse by her parents and went on to take lessons and enter riding competitions. Her house had spaces that were unusual for Christiana at the time—a huge playroom in the attic and a family room off the kitchen, where I might find her in the morning, before school, sitting on a soft sofa, sore from her riding lessons the day before.

In contrast, Maggie Rivers and her parents and sisters camped out in the basement of their small ranch-style house which was always under construction, never finished, at the end of Brown's Lane behind the school. The cinderblock walls offered a cool refuge from the summer heat, but always smelled like wet cement. Bobbie Sue Harvey lived in a nineteenth-century farmhouse, her backyard a maze of pigpens and chicken coops. Her parents, very gray and old, had produced a strikingly handsome blond son a few years older than Bobbie Sue and me, reminding me of another odd pair, Mrs. TG and Johnny. Most of my friends occupied houses that had been built in the nineteenth or early twentieth century, dwellings with low ceilings and dark, small rooms that contrasted with those in my own house. Only once did I enter the home of a black family on Brown's Lane. One holiday season the school sponsored a canned-food drive for the struggling families of the community, and I was deputized as Lady Bountiful to deliver the groceries to the needy. I managed to step just inside the front door and catch a whiff of kerosene before the occupants accepted the goods and I turned and left, still curious.

Christiana, then, made up a diverse society unto itself, but it appeared to me that the Phelpses remained outliers in their own land. Together, my parents always seemed to be looking over their shoulders, anxious because they occupied an outpost of middle-class respectability set in a hinterland that had a decidedly down-at-the-heels cast to it. Only much later would I come to understand the peculiar historical trajectories of my parents' respective kin networks, and the forces that came together to make them wary of Christiana and all that it represented—that is, the forces of downward mobility.

Every once in a while we would drive ten minutes to the east, out Hare's Corner Road, to visit the New Castle Farmers Market, a large indoor flea market owned by a Philadelphia businessman but patronized mainly by white southern migrants. We went as outsiders, as observers, and not as people who relied on the place for our clothes, food, or housewares. My father did enjoy the Delaware Valley specialties that he could buy from the Pennsylvania Dutch delicatessen counter staffed by Mennonite men and women—the souse (meat scraps suspended in gelatin) and scrapple. Yet we were aware of the fact that we were rubbing elbows with people different from us. We parked our station wagon next to their pickup trucks and souped-up sedans. We wore cotton slacks and plaid shirts, not denim overalls and T-shirts. For us, the Farmers Market represented a form of entertainment.

Thus we bore a curious relation to the town. We were not only in it but also of it, because my parents were so active in church and school politics. At the same time we cherished the belief that we were a family apart. As if to heighten the distance between ourselves and the rest of the town, my parents almost never walked anywhere; they drove to church and to Baldwin's market, though these places were only an eighth or a mile or so from our house. I did walk to school every day, but just once a year did I venture out on foot at night—on Halloween. Terribly nearsighted, I had to remove my glasses in order to fit my mask over my face, and as a result I relied on friends to take me by the hand and drag me from one front stoop to another. Even this precaution did not keep me from once falling in the stream that ran between my grandparents' house and the Bergers. But the evening remained a blur, and a frightening one at that, the faces of the "treaters" in the doorways indistinguishable from one another. In any case, together as a family, we preferred to see Christiana from the windows of our station wagon.

As it turned out though, in their effort to keep arm's-length from the idea as well as the town of Christiana, my parents could not always count on much help from me. Compared to our household, the town was a veritable carnival, a riotous place of love and longing.

The author's maternal grandmother, Clara Maria Chapin, c. 1898.

The author's maternal grandfather, Henry Arthur Phelps, c. 1898.

The author's paternal grandmother, Letitia Southard, and her brother, Philip Southard, c. 1907.

The author's father, Albert Hyatt Jones, Jr. (on the left), and his brother, William Southard Jones, c. 1924.

The author's paternal grandfather, Albert Hyatt Jones, Sr., and his mother, Susan McConnell Jones, c. 1935, Wilmington, Delaware.

The Phelps siblings and their mother, Hazleton, Pennsylvania, 1919. Front row from left to right: Alice, Henry, Katherine, Lois, Rachel, Ruth, Marion. Back row: a baby nurse holding the author's mother, Sylvia, and Clara Phelps (author's maternal grandmother).

The Phelps family at their home in Christiana, c. 1934. Front row, left to right: Marion, Lois, Sylvia, Rachel, Katherine. Back row: Alice, Henry Arthur Phelps (father), Henry, Clara Phelps (mother), Ruth.

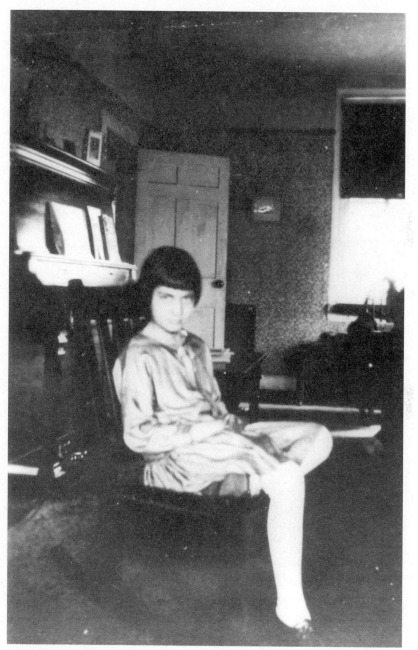

The author's mother, Sylvia Esther Phelps, c. 1928, Christiana, Delaware.

The author's father, Tech. Sgt. Albert H. Jones, Jr., c. 1945.

The author's father's brother, William Southard Jones, c. 1945.

Inspection before a test flight, Twentieth Air Force, 498 Bomber Group, 1945, Saipan. The author's father is third from right.

The author's father at work on the gun turret of a B-29, 1945, Saipan.

The 498 Bomber Group on the eve of its last mission over Japan, Summer, 1945, Saipan. The author's father is kneeling, far right.

The author's father's brother's bride, Dorothy Taylor Jones (far left), the author's parents, Sylvia Phelps and Albert Jones, and the author's paternal grandmother, Letitia Jones, 1945, Wilmington.

Wedding party at the bride's home in Christiana, Sept. 15, 1945. From left: the bride's sister Lois, bride's parents, Henry and Clara Phelps, the bride and groom, and the groom's mother, Letitia Jones.

The author, 1952.

The cousins: photo from a Phelps family Christmas card, 1950, Newport, Delaware. Front row, left to right: Elizabeth (Betsy) Phelps and Mary Ann Warner. Back row: Melvin Warner holding his sister Harriet, Nancy Phelps, Jean Phelps, the author, and Frederick (Ricky) Justis.

The author, 1952, at Mount Vernon, Virginia.

The Jones house on East Main Street, Christiana, c. 1960.

The author, her Jones aunt, and three of her Jones cousins. From left: Dorothy Jones, Bruce Jones, William Southard Jones, Jr. (Chip), the author, Barry Jones, and the author's paternal grandmother, Letitia Jones.

The author's aunt (Ruth, on right) with her new Buick, 1966, Christiana. On left is Ruth's first cousin, Esther Chapin Aiken.

The author's parents and her brother Kent Albert Jones, c. 1958, Christiana.

On the boardwalk: Spring, 1957, Ocean City, Maryland. The author's brother Kent, father, and brother Randall Arthur (Randy) (in stroller).

The author's brothers, Kent and Randy, 1957, Christiana.

The author and her brothers, Kent and Randy, 1959.

A swim in the pond: Roderick (Roddy) Justis and Kent and Randy Jones, 1961, Christiana.

The Phelps grandchildren, 1959, Christiana. Back row: Jean Phelps, Nancy Phelps, Betsy Phelps, Melvin Warner, Mary Ann Warner. Middle row: Roddy Justis, Harriet Warner, Ricky Justis. Front row: the author (kneeling), Randy Jones, and Kent Jones (in hat).

The author's brothers, Randy and Kent, and family dog (Mac), 1962, Christiana.

The author and her family, 2000, Wellesley, Massachusetts. Left to right: Anna Abramson, the author, Jeffrey Abramson, and Sarah Abramson.

3

Razzle-Dazzle

A few days after Labor Day in 1956, Janetta Jackson walked into Mrs. Preston's classroom and, in the process, wrought a quiet revolution. Still, the racial integration of Christiana-Salem Elementary School hardly went unnoticed. For months I had been overhearing the grown-ups talk about the mysterious newcomers who would soon start coming to the small, eight-grade school that drew pupils from the town and the surrounding countryside. Like the handful of other black children who entered Christiana that fall, Nettie lived directly behind the school playground, on Brown's Lane. Before that she had been bused to an all-black school, Absalom Jones, near Wilmington.

Together, Nettie and her cousin Freddie Rolfe, who entered second grade that year, formed a wedge that gradually opened up my school to other black children in the town. In the years immediately following the 1954 Supreme Court school desegregation decision, many Delaware districts instituted what they called a "school choice plan" in order to "allow" black pupils to continue to attend segregated schools if they chose to do so. In Wilmington, African American leaders lamented that, after a hard fight to challenge all-white public schools, some parents persisted in sending their children to all-black Howard High, by 1954 the only black high school in the entire state.

Years later, Nettie Jackson recalled that her friends were still making the long bus ride to Absalom Jones every day while she was making the hundred-yard dash from her backyard to the school door just before the bell rang. Nettie's mother had had little patience with their reluctant neighbors, but had acknowledged to her daughter that these black men and women feared for their children—that is, they feared the effects of rejection, of condescension. Some parents acted both instinctively and rationally, then, in hesitating before sending their children to a school where they might be made to feel inferior, different, unwanted.[1]

Within a year, however, the public bus that transported these children to Absalom Jones ceased to service Christiana, and a few more black children entered the ranks of the "walkers" to the school. One of them was Leena Martin, who joined our fourth-grade class in 1957.

My initial impressions of both Nettie and Leena reflected my self-absorption as an eight-year-old. Nettie's skin was light brown, and she had shoulder-length hair that she wore in braids fastened with the same kinds of barrettes that I used to fasten mine—pink and blue plastic birds and bows. Her mother was the daughter of the pastor of the local Mount Pleasant African Methodist Episcopal Zion Church (he also ministered to congregations in Newark, Delaware City, and Smyrna); her father worked for DuPont. I did not know it at the time, but he remained in General Services for as long as he worked for the company, the division my father had been able to leave behind after a couple of years by virtue of his white skin. Nettie grew up in a large extended family—her mother had seven brothers and six sisters, each of whom had an average of five children. Later asked how many of her cousins lived nearby, she replied, "Too many."

In contrast, Leena, who was very black, wore her hair in several short tight little braids that covered her head. Her parents were Brown's Lane renters, not homeowners like Nettie's. The fact that she had beautiful handwriting made me suspicious of her, for I had already developed a competitive streak that made me jealous of the talents of my classmates.

Delaware was one of the original defendants in the *Brown vs. the Board of Education* Supreme Court case of 1954. Its revised constitution of 1897 had mandated the racial segregation of all public school pupils, and black schools were manifestly unequal to their white counterparts. Some other states relied either on generations' worth of "custom" or on patterns of residential segregation to maintain separate and unequal schools for whites and blacks. As early as 1821 Delaware was taking no chances that children of the two races might someday learn together under the same roof: the legislature wrote racial prejudice into its code of laws. In 1950, the state was still levying two separate public-school taxes—one on blacks and the other on whites—ensuring that black schools would remained underfunded and understaffed.

Wilmington was the hometown of a number of well-known black activists in the nineteenth and twentieth centuries, including Mary Ann Shadd, the first black female newspaper editor in North America; Alice Dunbar-Nelson, a writer and political activist; and Louis P. Redding, a lawyer educated at Harvard Law School and the driving force behind the local Delaware legal challenges that eventually became part of the *Brown* case. Black leaders had early denounced discriminatory school laws. The Rev. Theophilous G. Stewart, speaking at Wilmington's Bethel African Methodist Church in 1882, offered an observation that was at once commonsensical and revolutionary: "Since the common schools belong to the State, and the State is composed of the people living in it, therefore all the people are joint stock owners in the common schools. The colored people are equal owners with the whites; all are beneficiaries. Any opposition to *equal* and unrestricted use of the common school is in direct opposition to their rights, made clear to all in the 14th Amendment."[2]

Yet change came slowly to Delaware. In 1950 the University of Delaware became the country's first institution of higher learning to be integrated as a result of a court order. Four years later, Louis P. Redding and Jack Greenberg, working under the auspices of the NAACP, managed to bring Delaware's uniquely discriminatory school system to the attention of the United States Supreme Court.[3]

The first black school in Christiana had been founded in the early 1870s with financial assistance provided by the Delaware Association for the Moral Improvement and Education of the Colored People, a group of Wilmington Quakers who sponsored a number of schools for African American children throughout the state during the period immediately after the Civil War.[4] Like most other black schools, Christiana 111-C was open only four months of the year, and it remained very small. In 1886 it had twenty-one students, limping along each year with only $70 from the state "colored fund" and less than $20 from local taxes. Teacher turnover was high because the salary—a dollar a day—was considerably lower than the state average, even for black schools.

In the early twentieth century, Delaware native Pierre S. DuPont decided to build a network of small schools for blacks throughout the state, including in Christiana. In this endeavor he followed the lead of other philanthropists of the time, most notably John D. Rockefeller Sr. and Julius Rosenwald, who established foundations to fund rural schools. DuPont himself personally dedicated the new structure for 111-C in 1920. Its $20,000 cost made it "one of the most expensive one-room school buildings in the nation," and it became, rather incongruously, a Christiana "showpiece," with electricity, running water, "and scientifically designed lighting, heating, and ventilation."[5] The white pupils, schooled in a nearby brown frame building constructed in the late nineteenth century, cast an envious eye at 111-C, which was rumored (falsely) to have flush toilets.

In the late 1920s, DuPont also oversaw the renovation of Howard High School (grades seven through twelve), a regional school located in Wilmington. Howard was famous for its classical curriculum (Alice Dunbar-Nelson taught literature there in the late teens), and for the black artists, scholars, musicians, and activists who at one time or another spoke or performed there, including Booker T. Washington, W. E. B. Du Bois, Paul Robeson, Alain Locke and Marian Anderson.[6] However, with the infusion of DuPont money, the faculty felt pressured to focus more on trade, or vocational, education, in effect downgrading Howard's role as a conduit for students out of Wilmington and into Ivy League universities.

The state provided no bus service to Howard, and most Christiana black children probably ended their schooling with grade seven. By 1947, only sixteen students were attending 111-C. It closed in 1952, and the state sent the remaining boys and girls (including Nettie and Leena) to Absalom Jones in Belvedere, west of Wilmington. (The school was named for the first black priest in the Protestant Episcopal Church; he had been born a slave in Sussex County in 1747, and, as a free man, had helped to found the African Free Society of Philadelphia in 1787.) Resources at Absalom Jones were decidedly inferior to those at the Christiana white school. Nettie Jackson remembered making do with textbooks that were so old they lacked the dates for famous people long since dead ("b. 1850–d.——").

Court cases challenging Delaware's system of segregated schools, combined with similar cases from Kansas, South Carolina, and Virginia, were consolidated to form what became known as *Brown vs. Board*. Two recent Delaware cases, *Bulah* (focusing on the town of Hockessin) and *Belton* (Claymont) had addressed the precedent established by *Plessy vs. Ferguson* (permitting "equal" segregated public facilities) in 1896. These two cases stressed the glaring inequality of black and white schools, rather than calling into question the principle of segregation *per se*. Representing Delaware before the Supreme Court in 1954, the state's Attorney General, Albert Young, argued against school integration on the grounds that white people's prejudices, and the resulting racial "tensions," were sufficient reason to keep the two groups of children apart from one another. As a Constitutional argument, this claim was weak. As a statement of the state's historic reasoning, however, it was both succinct and accurate.[7]

In 1955, the black residents of Christiana petitioned the Delaware State Board of Education, demanding that their children be allowed to attend the public school that was literally in their own backyard. A year later the school that was now called Christiana-Salem Elementary officially opened its doors to black students. Mrs. Preston assigned Nettie a desk along with the rest of the class and a new school year began. In Christiana, school integration did not alter the rhythm of town life. The firehouse remained an all-white institution, and only white kids crowded Baldwin's store after school.

The apparent equanimity with which Nettie and her cousin and a few others were ushered into the school stands in striking contrast to the controversy that had erupted downstate in Milford (population 5,200) a few years earlier. There a decision by the local school board to integrate the tenth grade of the all-white high school at the beginning of the school year (on September 8, 1954) had provoked bitter resistance from many, but not all, white parents. Within a few days a majority of whites had withdrawn their children from the public system in protest.

The conflict in Milford mirrored Delaware's heritage of obstruction in the area of black civil rights. The state had refused to ratify the Thirteenth, Fourteenth, and Fifteenth amendments, and its slaves were among the very last in the nation to be liberated from bondage. Legally, at least, slaves in Georgia had gained their freedom (in January, 1863, with the Emancipation Proclamation) before slaves in Delaware (in December, 1865, with the ratification of the Thirteenth Amendment).

Complicating the Milford picture was the appearance of the rabble-rousing founder of the National Association for the Advancement of White People, Bryant Bowles. Sensing a whole new field of labor, Bowles left his home in Washington D.C. to travel the short distance across the Delmarva Peninsula to Milford, where he set up temporary residence and harangued anxious crowds of whites with the defiant declaration, "The Negro will never be satisfied until he moves into the front bedroom of the white man's home, and when he tries that a lot of gunpowder will burn."

In Milford, at least, this form of boilerplate demagoguery masked deeper fears among whites that their children would be sharing classroom space with the children of black migrant workers housed in nearby labor camps during the spring and fall months. Not far from the town, the small farmers of isolated rural enclaves, fertile areas drained by small rivers and called "the Necks"—Cedar Neck, Slaughter Neck, and Milford Neck—maintained an overt defiance to the prospect of racial integration. These farmers, together with other white activists in Milford, launched an economic boycott against local store owners who continued to send their children to the newly integrated school.

Downstate black clergymen, members of the local NAACP, and the staff of the national NAACP Legal Defense Fund all registered their outrage over white defiance in Milford. Nevertheless, state officials, including the governor, judges on the state's highest court, and members of the state school board, signaled that foot-dragging would be the official Delaware response to the *Brown* decision. A newly constituted Milford school board, under pressure from a coalition of local white groups—parents, clergymen, teachers in the high school, and Democratic candidates for office—ordered the black students to return to their all-black high school, and the Milford system remained segregated for another thirteen years.[8]

It should be noted here that Christiana offered up no model of racial egalitarianism. Prejudice constituted a way of life there no less insidious because it was rarely directly remarked upon. The Phelpses casually invoked racist sayings: "Come eat at the white folks' table" meant "join the group"; and the "nigger in the woodpile" referred to some small but unwelcome fact that spoiled an otherwise pleasant situation. Nettie and I became friends but we never visited in each other's homes. My parents told me that they regretted that we must abide by a traditional code of racial etiquette now, though, they added, things might change in the future. I was therefore confused when a black family had a flat tire on the road in front of our house one day and my father pulled the tools out of his own car and helped them change it. He seemed genuinely solicitous of their welfare, and I had a hard time reconciling his role of Good Samaritan with his and my mother's deference to Christiana's white mores.

The town had a distinctly southern feel to it, and considering the drawls of migrants, a distinctly southern sound to it. Families from Tennessee in particular had been drawn to the area by the Chrysler assembly plant in Newark, by the General Motors plant in Wilmington, and by a variety of other New Castle manufacturing establishments, large and small, from paper mills to steel mills, and cardboard and can factories. These industries stood as testament to the economic vitality and diversity of manufacturing in the Brandywine Valley, beginning in the nineteenth century. Like most of its Deep-South counterparts, Christiana refrained from making any dramatic changes at all after the *Brown* decision. The Supreme Court's weak-kneed "implementation decree" ("*Brown II,*" released in December, 1955) ordering that districts must desegregate "with all deliberate speed," gave the town license to stall for another year and a half. Finally, in the fall of 1956, the school board agreed to admit black pupils, but only after being prodded into action by the black parents themselves.

I can only speculate why the whites who lived in Christiana exhibited no dramatic, concerted opposition to school integration. It is possible that at least some simply felt that *Brown* had ushered in a new era and that the law was long overdue, or at least that the law must be obeyed. Perhaps the small numbers of black students involved—no more than one or two per grade—and perhaps the fact that they were so young—no older than thirteen or so—helped to ease the transition. In contrast, the Milford district included a total of almost 2,000 students, and white parents seemed fixated on the specter of interracial dating. The physical proximity of Christiana's tiny black population to the school highlighted the palpable unfairness of transporting these children several miles away. Their presence offered no direct challenge to the town's social order—or rather social disorder, since leadership was so scattered. No single group of whites—neither the two white ministers nor their congregations, neither the parents nor the teachers, neither the firemen nor the firehouse ladies' auxiliary, not even the local school board—sought to block desegregation. The town was too small and out-of-the-way to attract the attention of opportunistic outsiders from other parts of the state or region, and no Democratic politicians bothered to block the doorway of the school; the potential votes just were not there. Because so many of the whites came from modest circumstances, they had no clear-cut economic privileges to preserve. In contrast, in

Milford, white landowners could easily conflate their class interests with their sense of "racial" superiority vis-à-vis the migrant workers.

I can speak with more authority about my own Phelpsian reaction to Nettie and Leena (and the few black kids from other grades I encountered on the playground every day at recess). By Phelpsian I mean not some sort of bland New England racial tolerance, but just the opposite; as a child my whole outlook on life was conditioned by a hypersensitivity to social difference. Therefore, a darker skin color represented just one more social signifier that set people apart from one another. My friend Lorena Lown, a native of Nashville, spoke with a heavy southern accent and attended the Salem Methodist Church; my friend Maggie Dalton went to the Christiana Methodist Church, and her father worked for Chrysler; my friends Janet Poroski and Teddy Lankowski were Polish American Roman Catholics; my friend Bobbie Sue Harvey lived on a working farm and ate fried dumplings for dinner. The kids hailing from Salem, a rural hamlet three or four miles west of Christiana, went home by bus, while town kids like me were walkers.

Even before I met my African American classmates, then, I was conscious of the way the town had been bisected, and then quadrisected, by the two great dividing lines, religion and class. The white Methodist minister spoke with a southern accent, and I heard rumors that he conducted worship services where people sang too loud. I associated his congregation with working-class families, and the Presbyterians with professionals like my father (though these crude distinctions, I realize in hindsight, were not wholly accurate).

Social difference assumed a tangible quality according to the jobs performed by my father in contrast to the jobs performed by the fathers of my friends. My father wore a suit and a hat to work; he sat at a desk and used the telephone and an adding machine. He went to work every day, day in and day out, with the exception of a two-week vacation in the summer. My friends' fathers went to work early in the morning and came home early in the afternoon, or they went to work in the afternoon and came home late at night; they wore overalls and carried lunch bags. Every once in a while, I would stop in at a friend's house after school and see her father sitting in the kitchen. I knew that he had been "laid off," and although I didn't understand the term, I knew that we must turn down the sound on the TV so that we did not provoke him.

Janetta Jackson and Leena Martin were different from me, but then so was virtually everyone else, in some way or another.

Moreover, the two of them were hard to lump together. During recess Nettie and I would run over to the edge of the playground fence and say hello to her mother while she was hanging laundry on a line strung between the Jacksons' garage and back porch. Mrs. Jackson had her hair pressed straight, in a pageboy, and she wore an apron over her print cotton dress, like my mother did. Nettie had a single sibling, a little sister, who was a miniature version of herself. In school, Nettie and I soon discovered that we were both gossipy little busybodies and enjoyed each other's company.

I never became friends with Leena. She wore ragged hand-me-downs and came from a big family that was very poor. Her younger brother Sam, small for his age and also very black, was a trouble-maker. But my white friend Mary Ann Fitzgerald came from a similarly large and struggling family. It was her brother, Eddie, who attacked the fourth-grade teacher on the playground one day at recess time. Mrs. Littlefield wrestled him to the ground and kept him there until the principal came running out the door and managed to pry the two of them apart. (My fifth-grade classmates and I rose out of our seats as one and rushed to the windows on the side of our room so that we could better view this shocking, delicious spectacle.) At Christiana-Salem Elementary School, Leena and her family had no monopoly on poverty, and her brother had no monopoly on belligerent behavior.

In the classroom, with her deep voice and her quiet demeanor, Leena maintained a detached aloofness, a reserve, that I found unnerving. She seemed older than her years, contemptuous of the foolishness that went on around her. I remember one day watching her on the playground as she tentatively joined in a game of tag. She was trying not to have a good time, but her face, showing a shy smile of delight, betrayed her. Secretly, I felt triumphant that we had brought her down to our level—that she could play this stupid little game and have a good time like the rest of us.

My mother provided me with a direct link to the school's history. She had attended the school when it was perched on the "back hill" running up from East Main Street to North Old Baltimore Pike, just below the Presbyterian Church. In the 1920s the school had employed two teachers (one upstairs and one downstairs) who taught four grades each. The two women (for they were always women) became skilled in maneuvering the pupils in one grade to the front of the room to use the blackboard and conduct recitations, while the other three grades worked independently at their desks.

By the 1950s, the school boasted grander quarters: a principal's office, a gym/auditorium, and indoor plumbing, but still offered little more than the bare-bones basics. It had no kindergarten; no music, art, or gym teachers; no cafeteria or library. Art classes consisted of spreading our desks with newspapers and using poster paints to cover large pieces of cream-colored paper on days too rainy to go outside. Music classes consisted of two grades squeezing into one classroom and singing as Mrs. Littlefield banged out "The Battle Hymn of the Republic" and then "Dixie," "The Erie Canal" then "Eating Goober Peas," and ended with rousing renditions of "America the Beautiful" and "The Star-spangled Banner." Only later did I appreciate that her playing represented an ecumenical salute to Delaware's border-state heritage.

Until 1959, Christiana-Salem existed as an independent school district, with only one school. Pupils who continued their education beyond eighth grade took a bus to Newark High School. Although only five miles away, it was light-years away in terms of size and resources.

When I entered first grade in 1954, the school had about 250 pupils, one classroom per grade, with twenty-five to forty-five pupils each. Despite its bland exterior and the predictable routine that went on inside—the recitation of multiplication tables and the droning of passages from "Dick and Jane" readers—the school was a place of high drama and deep emotions for me. It was not just that the world intruded into the classroom; the world *was* the classroom, and I encountered there a depth of feeling that contrasted mightily with the subdued atmosphere of home. Each day, Monday through Friday, I stepped into another scene, one with ever-shifting characters, stock villains and angels of mercy who ad-libbed their lines. It did not take long for me to understand that going to school was a kind of performance, and part of the excitement was not knowing from one day to the next whether I was to be part of the audience or part of the cast.

I vividly remember the first day of first grade, when, outfitted in a dress my mother had made me—a dark-blue shirtwaist patterned with sleepy little men in sombreros—I was informed by my teacher Mrs. Fetzer, a kindly lady with brown braids wrapped around her head, that she would be calling me by my full name, Jacqueline, and not by my nickname. Since my brother and my parents usually called me Jack, with the use of Jacqueline reserved for the times when I was punished for some misdeed, I felt stricken by her decision to call me "out of my name."

The second day of school is also etched in my memory. Stopping at Joanie Berger's house so that we could walk to school together, I found that I was too late and she had left without me. Though she was still in her pajamas, Mrs. Berger decided it was her duty to walk— or rather run—me up to the Corner herself. And so she did, her slippers flopping, her bathrobe flapping in the wind. I was simultaneously delighted and mortified at being part of this odd duo. Clearly I was emerging from the protective cocoon of Phelpsdom into a wider and more interesting world.

My teachers, each presiding over a single grade for a full year, ran the gamut of types, physical and otherwise. Four lived outside the town, and none attended the Presbyterian Church. Mrs. Petrocelli (second grade) represented evil incarnate (more about her later) while the rest indulged in varying degrees of kindliness, with Mrs. Preston (third grade) bordering on daffiness. As a Christiana institution, the school was definitely cosmopolitan. Mrs. Littlefield (fourth grade) was married to a part-time preacher in a small, religious sect of indeterminate origin. Mrs. O'Malley (fifth grade) made it a point to keep her Roman Catholic faith to herself, except the day after Pope Pius XII died, when she could not restrain herself from delivering this brief eulogy to the class: The pope, she said, had never done anyone any harm. Even at the time I thought she could have probably offered up a testimonial that was a bit more compelling.

Mrs. O'Malley was ancient, her white hair resisting black bobby pins all over, while Miss Morehead (sixth grade) was young and pretty, arriving each day with her lips ruby-red and her ears adorned with big clip-ons. Likewise, the two principals who served at the school during the decade afforded fascinating case studies. The formidable Miss Condry (parents and children alike used the evocative phrase "Battle Ax" to describe her) was rumored to have once punished a pupil by hanging her upside down in the office and cackling while the blood flowed out of the poor girl's ears. (No doubt the victim's underpants showed while she was in this dreadful condition—in my mind a fate worse than the physical discomfort she suffered.) In 1957 Miss Condry retired and within a couple of years was replaced by Mr. Peeler, who became a fast friend of our family. Mr. Peeler seemed to exist in a perpetual state of anxiety, his nerves frayed and his hands rendered uncontrollable by a bad cigarette-and-coffee habit. However, he and his family joined our church, a breakthrough of sorts as far as I was concerned. Now the Presbyterians had a lock on the school hierarchy.

Sandwiched between these two principals for a brief period was a rotund, flush-faced man from Pennsylvania who took the job only to be let go within a few weeks, accused by a couple of the girls of molesting them. About this time that I noticed that the school janitor had also ceased to report for work. My queries yielded only the cryptic reply that he had been fired for doing bad things to girls in the janitor's closet. With its huge sink and jumble of mops, brooms, and buckets, the janitor's closet seemed to be a unlikely place for activity of any kind, let alone something that involved more than one person. I was mystified.

At school, then, the novelty of the classroom, lunchroom, and playground served as an alternately delightful and frightful counterbalance to my homey, Phelpsian routine.

On the playground, I knew exhilaration intermingled with physical pain: For such a poor, little school, we enjoyed an impressive variety of equipment. Yet by today's standards, the playground was a minefield, littered with many contraptions that routinely inflicted physical harm upon those who so innocently tore out the back door at recess. The seesaws were long, hulking, splintery wooden planks, and it was only a matter of time before anyone who maneuvered her end down to the ground wriggled off and let her "playmate" come crashing down—the seesaw as weapon of destruction, or at least instrument of torture. Likewise, the rusty steel merry-go-round was safe enough when used the way it was intended. But we managed to twist it into a hazard for unsuspecting younger kids by pushing it so fast they stumbled, fell, and then were either dragged until their knees were bloody, or faced some more dire fate by getting caught underneath it. On the playground, Darwin ruled: Chronological age mattered less than physical strength and raw courage.

The playground's crowning glory though was the razzle-dazzle, a piece of equipment that was literally breathtaking in its effect on us.

(In the year 2000, when two fifty-year-olds reminisced about their days at the school in the 1950s, they agreed that riding the razzle-dazzle was the single experience they remembered most vividly and most fondly.) It consisted of a long steel pole capped with a hoop-like circle that held eight long dangling chains. Attached at the bottom of each chain was a two-tiered rectangular wooden handle that hung about four feet off the ground. When used as it was intended to be used, with eight kids loping around in a circle, the razzle-dazzle offered a sedate kind of fun—the point was to lift your feet off the ground and hang by the handles as the overhead circle continued to be turned by your playmates. But no one was content to do that for very long.

Instead, we devised our own thrills and turned the razzle-dazzle into a maypole from hell. One person would hold onto the wooden handle and then stay back, allowing three or four others to proceed under and ahead of her, so that, at the appointed time, with everyone else running as fast as possible, she could jump into the air while holding on for dear life. If everyone cooperated, the lucky kid could swing out and up as high as six feet off the ground. The girls especially were a sight to behold: Our blouses, loosed from skirt waistbands, waving like flags in the wind; our bloody knees on display for all to see as we whirled around and around.

A really good ride often preceded a fall. If you were high enough you had no choice but to let go of the handle and travel a considerable distance through the air before landing on your back and suffering any number of consequences—the breath knocked out of you, dizziness, scrapes and bruises. The teachers on playground duty observed all of this with studied indifference, since the whole concept of recess safety was still many years off. In the meantime, I knew what it felt like to fly.

I had the calloused palms to prove that I was tall for my age and often won the twice-daily race out the back door to the razzle-dazzle, for when the bell rang, everyone headed straight for the pole, and the smaller and weaker ones were consigned to the monkey bars and the seesaws. After a streak of good weather and many consecutive days on the playground, my callouses would turn to blisters, and the blisters would break and leave open sores that made writing painful—my own little pus-pocket badges of courage.

But at school I also came to know hatred: My second-grade teacher, Mrs. Petrocelli, commuted each day from her home in a fashionable upper-middle-class suburb north of Wilmington, apparently for the sole purpose of tormenting herself and thirty wretched pupils in Christiana Elementary School. She wore high heels and glittering, shimmering dark green and purple rayon dresses, as if to remind us that she might be in this poor town, but she certainly was not of it. She expressed her contempt for us with every breath she took, using a handkerchief on the knob of the classroom door, so that she would not suffer contamination from such close proximity to snot-nosed seven-year-olds. Preoccupied with the source of unpleasant odors in the classroom, she routinely conducted interrogations of individuals in the hallway: Did you produce that smell because you have to go to the bathroom? (Leonard Laster achieved cult status among the rest of us when one day he stuttered, trembling with fear, "Nothing stank in here until you walked into the room.")

The accursed child who incurred her wrath for a particular offense could count on feeling her long, blood-red, pointy thumbnail dig into his chin, as she slowly shook his head from side to side while lecturing on the fine points of classroom decorum. She was known to greet new kids who just moved to the town with the public announcement to the class, "We are all very sorry that you have come to our school."

By this time my father was on the town school board, and I enjoyed a certain degree of insulation from her excesses. (Indeed, Mrs. Petrocelli conveniently disappeared off the school payroll the year before my brother entered second grade.) Yet my heart went out to my friend, Donna Wilson, a mousy little girl who by her very meekness seemed to enrage Mrs. Petrocelli. Donna was as smart as the rest of us, and more compliant than most of us. That she was from a poor family seemed to give Mrs. Petrocelli license to ridicule and demean her in front of the rest of the class. In June I got the biggest shock of my young life when we received our report cards and Donna silently showed me hers; she was not allowed to advance to the third grade because she was being held back for another whole year. This was my first encounter with classroom injustice: Mrs. Petrocelli would have her sick kind of fun and Donna would continue to suffer in silence. On the last day of school, the annual class outing was supposed to have allowed me to finish the year on a triumphal note, but instead it was bittersweet: the June 14, 1956, "Christiana Calling" column written by my mother notes that "Mrs. [Petrocelli's] second graders hiked to the home of Jackie Jones to East Main Street," there to partake of a picnic by the pond. I had survived the year, but at considerable cost to my self-respect.

At school I also learned new forms of self-expression: On rainy days the pupils in Mrs. Preston's third-grade class had to stay in from recess, and we were forced to amuse ourselves with colored blocks and games like Parcheesi and dominoes. And then one day Lorena Lown, with her straight brown Dutch-boy cut and her soft, Tennessee drawl, decided that she would teach a few of us how to jitterbug, a dance she learned from her older sisters. As she sang "Mama's Little Baby Loves Shortnin', Shortnin', Mama's Little Baby Loves Shortnin' Bread," we paired off and swayed to the music she sang, holding right hands together, left hands around our partner's waist, pushing out and twirling. Mrs. Preston watched, disapproving, but at last I was learning what it felt like to put physical movements together with music.

Lorena stood in relation to me as a teacher of sorts, but usually I considered the Southerners to be exotic counterpoints to the Phelpses. I periodically lapsed into their way of talking, dropping the "ing" off words whenever possible, and, when my parents and teachers weren't listening, trying out the sound of "ain't," a word the Phelpses considered akin to an obscenity. At school I could slip on another identity for a few minutes to see how I liked the sound and feel of it before returning (inevitably, that night at the dinner table) to my more proper self.

In school I knew shame for the first time: No matter what the grade or teacher, I was a professional Goody Two-shoes, slavishly in pursuit of the good grades and official approval that would win me the crown as the *best girl in the class*. The fact that my father had become active on the Christiana school board did not go unnoticed among my teachers and no doubt smoothed the way for me. And so the appearance of a substitute teacher could cause me great consternation, simply because such an interloper had no preconceived notion of how compliant and eager to please I really was. One day in fourth grade I had to contend with a particularly stern woman who grew increasingly exasperated with my unruly classmates as the day went on. By the afternoon she was moved to announce that anyone who persisted in talking would be punished immediately. When Maggie Dalton leaned across the aisle to express her annoyance at this dictate, I whispered, "Don't talk to me!" But it was too late: before I knew it, I was standing in the corner at the front of the room, my face red with shame, there to languish until it was time to go home. My friends were amazed at my swift descent into bad-girl land, and the whole class no doubt rejoiced at this strange turn of events. As a group they felt moved to inform Mrs. Littlefield upon her return that I had been banished to the corner the day before. I took some consolation from the fact that she was incredulous, but even her sympathy could not erase the lifelong memory of that day for me.

I knew lust: The year was 1956, the place was Mrs. O'Malley's fifth-grade classroom, and I arrived at school wearing my first "tight skirt," a below-the-knee, red corduroy affair that, considering my bottom-heavy shape, made look like nothing so much as a well-dressed pear. However, I did manage to attract the attention of Marty Cobb. What Marty lacked in raw intelligence (he had been held back a few years and was eleven or twelve) he made up in striking good looks, his blond wavy hair swept up into a stunning ducktail. "Look at that red chick over there," I heard him say to a friend (I even remember where he was standing—he was leaning nonchalantly against the blackboard), and my life was forever changed. I was slipping away from the Phelps-land and into Jones territory.

I knew the anxiety that accompanies the negotiation of complex social groupings: Elementary school-age girls early gain sophistication in the kinds of social rituals that mark small communities—gossiping, expressing petty jealousies and resentments, provoking temporary feuds, somehow managing to preserve friendships. Considering the girls in the grade above me, in my grade, and the grade below as the set of potential friends, my relationships consisted of ever shifting subsets depending who had said what to whom the day before. A favorite ploy was for Eileen (for example) to say to me (for example): "Go say to Crystal, 'Eileen thinks she's smart, doesn't she?' [an all-purpose indictment meant to convey the subject's general obnoxiousness]; and then come back and tell me what she said." If Crystal said, "yes, Eileen *does* think she's *so* smart," you could count on the severance of that particular connection for at least the next forty-eight hours or so.

My status as an overachiever and as a member of the upright Phelps family took me only so far in the realm of afterschool politics, when we wended our way home, peeling off to each other's houses. In that regard I was at a distinct disadvantage compared to, say, Melinda Taylor, who early laid claim to the mantle of most popular girl. Melinda was the town roller-skating queen. She took weekly lessons at the Merry Land Roller Rink down on Route 40, not far from the Delaware-Maryland line, and she and her skating partner, a cute boy from another school, competed regularly in pairs exhibitions. The granddaughter of the owner of the liquor store at "the Corner," she put on airs, I thought, and lorded over the rest of us by inviting kids from out of town to her annual birthday parties held in the crepe-paper-festooned basement of her house on West Main Street. Consequently, I had to endure "Christiana Calling" notices like the one from February, 1959: "[Melinda Taylor] entertained a number of friends in honor of her 10th birthday last Friday at the home of her parents, Mr. and Mrs. [Walter Taylor].") My so-called best friends showed no compunction about shunning me after school if Melinda invited them to her place instead.

I felt I would forever remain at a disadvantage in the popularity department because I had no older siblings who might spread lurid tales about Elvis Presley or instruct the younger set in the intricacies of creating French twists or applying eyeliner. In this sense my two little brothers were a distinct liability, for the kids who partook most fully of afterschool life (it seemed to me) were the ones who went home to houses full of older brothers and sisters, boys and girls who knew the names of every Philadelphia high schooler to ever appear on *American Bandstand*. Lacking the broader knowledge that teenagers provided, I remained in a suspended state of childhood, always tagging along, never bullying or teasing the way younger siblings felt free to do when in the company of kids shorter than themselves.

In school I also learned revulsion: By the time I was ten, consolidation with the Newark public school district had conferred its mixed blessings on us. It had taken four separate public referenda to win the support of a majority of Christiana's voting taxpayers to achieve this move, since "progress" was viewed with suspicion by a goodly number of the town's residents. But now we had a music teacher who came once a week to lead us in singing in our classrooms, and my parents also paid to have her give me clarinet lessons. The insistent way she tapped her baton on the music stand, her other hand on her hip, her lips pursed and jaw clenched, signaled the mutual unhappiness and frustration that all my music teachers and I would inflict upon each other for years to come.

Now we also had a multipurpose room that served as gym, auditorium, and cafeteria, but the lady in charge of the cafeteria, Mrs. May Pickles, was not content to serve the food. She also assumed the

role of food police, emerging from behind the counter at the end of
the lunch period to make sure that we had consumed every last scrap
of the day's meal. I loved to buy lunch on special occasions, but
developed an aversion to the rice pudding that often accompanied
the sub sandwich or mound of spaghetti that I craved. After pushing
the thick, pale glob around with my spoon for a while, I would look
up to find Mrs. Pickles looming over me, her feet planted firmly on
the floor next to our stainless-steel picnic table, insisting that I remain in my place until I had downed all of the dreaded stuff. I
gagged, my face turning redder and redder, as I did her bidding and
at the same time consigned her to the same category of human being
as Mrs. Petrocelli.

In school I came face-to-face with terror: Well, I was supposed to, at
least. Throughout my elementary-school years (1954–60), we had
regular air-raid drills so that we could prepare ourselves should the
Soviet Union decide to obliterate all of the DuPont facilities in the
Delaware Valley. We did not doubt that the detonation of an atomic
bomb just down the road from us would cause some damage to both
buildings and bodies, but air raids were conducted as if the blast
would amount to little more than a bad tornado. At the sound of the
siren, we practiced how to march quietly, single-file, into the hallway,
where, lined up against the cinderblock walls we covered our heads
with our arms and kept our lips buttoned: THERE WILL BE NO TALK-
ING DURING A NUCLEAR HOLOCAUST.

It occurred to me that the Russians must be intent on attacking
during school hours, for at home no one ever discussed or worried
about the Bomb—that was a threat to the school, to us while we were
at school. Lying in bed at night, I would make a checklist of all the
canned goods my mother stored in the basement and wonder: which
would be worse? Dying from a nuclear blast, or surviving one if you
had nothing to eat nothing but canned green beans?

My generalized fears were not confined to the classroom and cinderblock hallways: while we were at church, we worried about going
to hell. In fact, church bore a striking similarity to school in many
respects. I understood that worshipping God was not the same as
learning to read and write, and yet these respective activities were not
necessarily central to my experiences at either place.

At church too I felt the stirrings of romantic longing, standing
outside on the sidewalk while I listened to the teenaged organist,
Alan Comer, play "Jesu, Joy of Man's Desiring" on the new double-

banked Hammond organ that my grandparents had donated to the congregation. As his slender fingers moved gracefully from one bank of keys to another, I was in danger of swooning from the sight and sound of his playing. And so God, music, and earth-bound love became inextricably linked in my mind.

There are other memories as well: the warmth of an autumn afternoon sun streaming through the stained glass vestibule windows, as the Homecoming crowd heaped their plates with chicken salad and filled their cups with steaming black coffee before filing back into the sanctuary to eat lunch in the pews; after Sunday morning service, the thrill of climbing atop the horsehair sofa located directly behind the preacher's lectern, and surveying the sanctuary from a new angle, always awed by the magnificent simplicity of the forty-foot-high ceilings and the smooth, plain white walls; the reassurance that emanated from the singing, the dirge-like sounds of the tiny congregation, voices raised in "Praise God from Whom All Blessings Flow;" and the opportunity to mingle with grown-ups after the service, a time when people of all ages came together for a few minutes each week, their conversation a prelude to the discussions I would hear at my grandmother's that afternoon—about plans for an upcoming fund-raising supper, comments about the renewed vitality of the Sunday School and the fine performance of the choir soloist that morning.

It was possible to participate actively in the church without feeling burdened, either time-wise or spirit-wise. Presbyterians were respectful of routine but scornful of ritual. Sunday morning services lasted exactly one hour (sometimes a couple of minutes less but rarely a couple of minutes more). I considered Sunday School as a place for earning awards and recognition. By the time I was twelve, I was the proud owner of a pin with five or six tiny bars attached like a ladder to the bottom of it, each bar a prize for year-long perfect attendance. Not until I was older and able to understand the fine points of Presbyterian theology—the so-called choices already predestined by God, the terrifying uncertainty of heaven or hell—did cosmic fear bear down heavily upon my soul.

Like school, church was a locus of my parents' public influence. My father especially made his mark on local politics through these two institutions. Beginning with his election to the Christiana school board in 1956, he rapidly ascended the ladder of lay educational leadership, becoming president of that board in 1957. He also served in various capacities in the church as an heir to the Phelps religious dynasty. My mother's father had been elected an elder in 1930, and beginning in the 1940s his daughters and sons-in-law began rotating among the positions of elder, trustee, Sunday School teacher, pianist, member of the cemetery committee, member of the visiting (fund-raising) committee, treasurer, choir member.

The net result of all of this school board and church activity was that my father was rarely home in the evening, his after-dinner hours consumed by meetings. At home, he spent a considerable amount of his time talking on the phone to would-be supporters for the impending showdown of the day. He served as a guiding force in the controversy over school consolidation, lobbying hard against the town folks' natural tendency toward inertia (in favor of static property taxes and the oldfangled education their children received).

My father existed in a constant state of politicking. He relished a good fight for its own sake, tracking the configuration and reconfiguration of alliances among the school-board or church players, their feuds based on personality as much as policy. His early dream of becoming a lawyer was dashed by a member of the Delaware bar who ridiculed his plans to go to law school at night (the state's legal establishment was a tight clique that disdained and discouraged poor-boy upstarts). Still, he developed an assertive public style that would have served him well in the courtroom. By day he sat in a drab office interviewing lower-level job candidates or punching numbers into an adding machine for a boss in Wilmington. By night he was a force to be reckoned with at school or at church in Christiana.

For my parents and all of Phelpsdom, local church politics was a constant source of preoccupation. In this regard the family was carrying on a time-honored tradition that had shaped the life of the congregation over the last two centuries. Within a few years of its founding in 1732, the earliest congregants had managed to scrape together enough money to erect a modest wooden frame structure. The first preacher was Charles Tennent, son of the Rev. William Tennent, who founded the Presbyterian "Log College" in New Jersey (later Princeton University). William presided over an illustrious family of ministers; all four of his sons were Presbyterian ministers who left their mark on congregations scattered in Pennsylvania, New Jersey, and Delaware.

During this period (of the First Great Awakening) Middle-Colony Presbyterians emerged as the rivals of the English Anglican (later Episcopal) Church and its agent in the colonies, the Society for the

Propagation of the Gospel in Foreign Parts. (Recognizing that the Scotch-Irish Presbyterians offered a political as well as a religious challenge to the church of the Crown, one SPG missionary denounced members of one Delaware congregation in 1728 as "Presbyterians by profession, of the most bigoted sort."[9]) In 1739, when the famous revivalist George Whitefield preached to a large crowd at Christiana Bridge, he was received with open arms by the "New Light" Charles Tennent, whose family embraced the Great Awakening religious enthusiasm in opposition to Anglican restraint. By the late eighteenth century however, the predominantly Scotch-Irish, commercial-minded Presbyterians were losing ground to the Methodists, who quickly became associated with downstate rural-agricultural interests. In the mid-twentieth century, the fact that Christiana boasted three different kinds of Methodist churches and only one Presbyterian testified to the loss of the town's original commercial orientation.

Despite its promising beginnings, the Christiana Presbyterian church always had a difficult time supporting its own minister. Over the years the congregation was forced either to share a minister with the Presbyterians in nearby White Clay Creek, Pencader, New Castle, Stanton, Newark, Head of Christiana, or Elkton, or to rely on the regional Presbyterian Board of Home Missions for a "stated supply" (i.e., temporary) minister. As late as 1950 the weekly salary amounted to only $25. These fill-in pastors were usually either retired and bound for glory soon, or young, right out of seminary and eager to move on to a more substantial congregation and a more predictable paycheck. Money, or rather the lack thereof, dictated the degree to which the congregation might receive weekly spiritual sustenance from a minister. In 1883, "because of the inability of the church to support a pastor, Mr. [James] Campbell, to relieve the church of pecuniary embarrassment, resigned." [10]

The lack of resources did not deter church members from either thinking or building in grandiose terms. In 1856 several prominent members had pledged enough money to build an impressive stucco building in the plain style of a medieval chapel. Yet at no time before 1950 or so did the number of members amount to more than fifty-five souls. This disjuncture between its substantial physical plant on the one hand and its small congregation on the other would remain a distinguishing feature of the church.

The Presbyterian form of governance was similar to that of the Congregationalists. Each congregation had a great deal of autonomy, and members were, as a matter of principle, resistant to dictates issued from on high—in this case, from the regional Presbytery consisting of a committee of clergy and laymen-elders, or from the United Presbyterian Church, a national body. Insulated from outside interference, members of the Christiana church felt free to squabble among themselves, and squabble they did. The locus of conflict shifted erratically among the two executive boards (the elders of the Session and members of the Board of Trustees), the cemetery committee (the graveyard was a source of revenue as well as a source of wrangling over fees and upkeep), the Ladies Aid Society, and the choir. Of this last group, one chronicler of the church's history noted, "It is a curious and unhappy fact that when trouble, or lack of harmony, arises in church, the choir is so often the storm centre."[11] Apparently the choir loft served as the base of operations for women who, shut out of formal positions of church leadership, challenged men who were choir directors, ministers, Sunday School directors, elders, and session members. Well into the twentieth century, ministers were still labelling the choir loft the "battleground of the church."

Church records indicate that the congregation lurched from one controversy to another—a "pew rent rebellion" in 1802, the reluctance of certain members to join a temperance society in 1835, and, throughout the nineteenth century, periodic church trials of accused adulterers, drinkers, gossips, liars, ladies who received male visitors in their homes after dark, Sabbath slackers (who preferred to attend cricket matches on Sunday), profaners of the Lord's name, and of course, the ubiquitous instigators of choir "disturbances." A series of sensational trials in 1872 resulted in the excommunication of thirteen members, leaving a total membership of twenty-four.

It is possible that at this point at least in their respective histories, the four churches of Christiana shared a great deal when it came to enforcing righteous behavior among their congregants. Presbyterians and Methodists in general tried to insist that members forego revelry and frivolity of all kinds. Indeed, one of the early complaints about the emerging Methodist code of behavior was that "God did not require so much strictness as the Methodists said He did" (this from an elderly Episcopalian in Lewes, Delaware).[12] Peter Spencer, the founder of the Union African Methodist Church, preached a spare doctrine of frugality, industry, and abstinence among blacks. Despite differences in church governance and musical styles (the Methodists were definitely more enthusiastic than the Presbyterians, and the black Methodists definitely more enthusiastic than the white Methodists), organized religion loomed large in the everyday lives of Christiana church members, black and white.

By the early twentieth century, the Presbyterian congregation was too small to excommunicate anyone, and the church found itself in receivership, under the guidance of a committee of clergy from Wilmington and Elkton. In the mid-1920s, one congregant could declare rather defensively that the church was in "good condition, with harmony and goodwill among its members, and while the number was small, harmony and happy relations are certainly a desirable asset to any church."[13]

Exacerbating a generally precarious situation was the fact that the small number of the church's governors had become an entrenched hierarchy. The Session consisted of four elders (all men) who served *de facto* if not *de jure* life terms, and the Board of Trustees included a self-perpetuating group responsible for tapping replacements for themselves. In some respects such rigidity was mandated by the size of the congregation—only a couple of dozen people, and fully half of them (the women) could not hold office in any case until the late 1940s. This state of affairs meant that officers often simply renominated a current member who was nearing completion of his three-year term. In 1907 they refused to accept the decision of one of their own who announced he would not run for a seventh consecutive term. So fearful were they of any instability on the board that they declared him the winner of a nonelection and installed him for another three years, bringing his length of service to twenty-one years.

After 1857, the fact that its territorial and building designs outstripped its resources meant that the church would have to become an aggressive fund-raising organization. On the eve of the Civil War, the Ladies of the Church hosted a supper in order to raise the $800 needed to furnish the new building. Thereafter much church activity was directed toward raising money—through ice cream socials, steamboat excursions to Cape May, choir concerts for the general public, lawn parties, literary readings, strawberry festivals, and chicken and oyster suppers. Efforts to borrow money from the Cemetery Fund added fuel to the fires of church feuding. In the 1920s the church instituted an annual Rally Day, a Sunday service intended to beg members and former members alike for money, and a Home coming Day (the second Sunday in October) intended to beg former members to contribute to the Cemetery Fund.

The chronically strapped state of the congregation meant that it was dependent upon the largesse of the national church for both general operating expenses and the minister's salary for much of its history. Turnover among peripatetic preachers took its toll on re ligious life. By the mid-twentieth century there existed no sustained clerical tradition in terms of Calvinist theology, the bedrock of Pres byterianism. Still, in 1949, an unlikely newcomer breathed new life into the church. Eighty years old, he had just completed a stint as a missionary to Korea, and he brought to Christiana the same zeal he had demonstrated on behalf of the benighted souls of Seoul. By this time, the Presbyterian church was drawing members from the mush rooming tract housing developments around Newark and Ogletown, households headed by skilled and middle-level white collar workers at Electric Hose and Rubber, Delaware Power and Light, the United States postal service, and, of course, the DuPont Company.

By this time too the Phelpses were not only providing the core of leadership for the church, but as a group they were also pumping relatively large amounts of money into it, winning for themselves the gratitude of the congregation though of course not necessarily guar anteeing themselves a spot in Calvinist heaven. When a missionary who took time off from harvesting souls in British Cameroon came to visit the church to solicit our prayers and our financial support, my family was granted the honor of hosting him for Sunday dinner. He took my finger measurement and later sent me a ring carved from elephant ivory, a priceless treasure that bespoke my elevated status as a Phelps as much as my spiritual connection with other Christians in a far-off corner of the world.

Our missionary-minister died in 1955, and he was replaced by a recent graduate of Princeton and the church's first full-time pastor in forty years. Liberal in his religious beliefs and restless in his ambi tions, this younger man left in 1959 to pursue a Ph.D. at Columbia University. By that time, membership had increased to 64, my father and one of my aunts were members of the Session, and another aunt was church treasurer. He was succeeded by a kindly man who startled the upright congregation with his informal demeanor—he smoked a pipe, loved to fish in the pond behind our house, drove an Opal (

real curiosity those days in Delaware), had a daughter who was cheerleader at Newark High School, and took his family to Sunday dinner at McDonald's. And yet he preached a stern Calvinism that would have made Jonathan Edwards proud, forcing me to contemplate the terrifying possibility that no matter how hard I tried to be good, God might have already decided that I wasn't worth bothering to save.

In the late 1950s the church began to deviate from its stubbornly insular history, and started to troll for new souls in the immediate vicinity of Christiana. With some prodding, church members reached out and formed connections: the Sunday School joined with the Methodists to offer Summer Bible School, the Ladies Aid Society became part of the national group called United Presbyterian Women as well as the interdenominational Church Women United, and congregants raised modest sums of money to sponsor missionaries in Japan and on Johns Island in South Carolina.

A Youth Canteen for town teenagers held on Saturday nights at the low, flat stucco Sunday School building produced a novel sight the next morning—the church parking lot littered with cigarette butts and a stray beer can or two. This refuse from the night before conjured up hoods in tight pants and black leather jackets sharing a smoke with girls in tight skirts and sweaters. Unfortunately, the Youth Canteen did not win many converts for the church, and this experiment in community outreach was abandoned by the time I was old enough to participate in it.

In 1959 I witnessed the beginning of a new and extraordinary tradition in Christiana—a Thanksgiving Day "union service" that brought together the town's four churches early in the morning, before the Newark High School football game in the afternoon. Each year thereafter the service would rotate among the four congregations, and it was with a certain amount of trepidation mingled with curiosity that I ventured out in the company of my brothers and my parents to church buildings that I had seen only from the outside for years.

One cold, bright Thanksgiving Day, I found myself in the small sanctuary of the UAME church, anxiously scanning the crowd for the few faces that I recognized. Since we were all Mid-Atlantic evangelical Protestants, the general order of services and even the hymns were familiar to me, but the demeanor of the congregation was not. As the black preacher welcomed everyone from the pulpit, I thought I heard unfamiliar sounds emanating from the pews—"Amen," and "yes, brother": *Someone was talking!* I froze, shocked at this breach in decorum: Would we all receive a reprimand for this incredibly rude behavior? In my own church on Sunday morning, worshippers sneezed and snorted, they coughed and sighed and sometimes even snored, they hushed restless young children, but no one ever dared to utter a word out loud. Later during the service, while the preacher was offering up his sermon, an all-purpose homily calculated to meet with everyone's approval, the calls from the congregation became more frequent, insistent, and loud—"Yes, it's so!"—and I wondered why no one had warned me about this strange performance ahead of time.

At my grandmother's house late that afternoon, the Phelpses gathered for post-turkey dessert, and commented only obliquely about the novel service that several of us had participated in a few hours earlier. After a brief foray into the local reaches of the denominational and racial diversity of American Protestantism, we retreated back into the fold, relieved to be home again. Still the union Thanksgiving Day service allowed us to be part of history for one day each year; after all, by 1960, southern black people were making headlines with their challenges to Jim Crow, and Freedom Riders and lunch-counter protesters were becoming staples on the evening news. But for the other 364 days of the year we smugly lived our separate lives, convinced that the drive for civil rights would have little real impact on the town of Christiana, on where people lived and whom they worked with. Anti-integration violence I thought was a southern phenomenon—the southern part of Delaware, the southern part of the country.

Each day, when I walked home from school, I embarked on a little journey of discrete steps and stages that reminded me who I was, where I had come from, and where I must return every afternoon. In the morning I half-ran the mile distance so that I would arrive before the bell rang, but in the afternoon the pace back home was more leisurely. At three o'clock I became a walker, distinguished from those who took the bus home, and I almost never visited the home of a bus rider; it was as if we lived in two separate worlds. A plaid-patterned aluminum lunchbox in one hand and a red plastic book-bag slung over a shoulder, I set out from school together with three or four friends. In a couple of minutes we arrived at Mr. Baldwin's store where the after-school trade in Snickers and Cokes was apparently enough to keep him in business. Crossing the intersection at the Corner, we passed by the Fire House and said hello to the three or four men, talking and laughing, sitting on folding chairs in front of the open bays, the shiny red engines at the ready. Then we wended our way down the street and, depending on the day, I might tarry at the house of Eileen Robb or Mary Ann Fitzgerald to watch TV, play a game of baseball, receive an impromptu dance lesson from their older sisters, or explore various deserted sheds, garages, and out- buildings. Then I would trudge on by myself, past the historical marker commemorating Lafayette's landing, and down to the bridge over the Christina, where the sidewalk ended.

I would take time to scramble down the bank to the water's edge and explore the underbrush, searching for the signs of human activity—a beer can tossed from a passing car, an abandoned fishing- tackle box, shells from a shotgun, a lone glove, the oar from a rowboat washed up on the bank. Rummaging around the creek bank afforded pleasures quite distinct from roaming around the woods and the pond in the back of our house. I loved to discover cast-off stuff, stinking and useless though it might be. The Christina itself showed no signs of life, with the exception of a garter snake slithering out from under the mud-matted weeds at the water's edge. Most of the time the river could not even muster a current. Still, its banks yielded precious artifacts, things doubly fascinating because no one else seemed to have the slightest interest in them.

I would then cross the bridge to my grandmother's house, where I would always find my Newark aunt; without children of her own, she had the time to visit her mother every afternoon. I would regale the two of them with tales of my recent successes in school, and my aunt would compliment me on keeping my white blouse so clean all day.

Finally I reached the end of the line for all walkers who headed east—my house. Gradually I had shed my friends along the way and now looked forward to a solitary ramble in the woods before dinner- time. No homework, music lessons, or after-school sports took up my afternoon-time. And following the excitement of school, coming home was a bit like going into a room and shutting the door.

4

Blood in the Salad

The little boy had been buried in a shallow grave, but before killing him his parents had tortured him by burning his body with cigarettes. The photo the magazine ran with the story showed a boy with close-cropped hair and sad eyes. When he died he was about the same age that I was when I read about him (ten years old), and yet he was my polar opposite. I was a girl; he was a boy. I came from a warm and secure home; he came from a place where the mother and father who had given birth to him took pleasure in his physical pain. I walked on the ground; he lay under it. I was living; he was dead.

My initial horror at this story soon evolved into a morbid fascination. I tried to imagine what it had been like for him just before he died: What were the sounds and smells of cigarettes burning his flesh? Had he cried? Did he die quickly or slowly and in agony, crying for help? Was his face moist with tears? I seemed to have an obligation (to myself, to him?) to ponder these things, to make myself think about them when I became too complacent, too caught up in the banal happiness of my everyday life.

I developed a habit, a bad one, that summer I first read the story. I began to set apart a certain time of every day—the hours after dinner, before darkness fell—to remember the little boy and to reconstruct in my mind as vividly as I could his last few minutes on earth. As the last dishes from dinner were washed and the family quietly dispersed—my father to a church or school-board meeting, my mother to read the newspaper or finish her chores, my brothers to play outside in the twilight—I would think about death, the nothingness that awaited us all. For years afterwards, I could not make it through an evening in late July without feeling a dread that was so deep and mysterious I had absolutely no idea what to do with it. Yet each day, by the time morning came, I had won for myself another brief reprieve.

118

Perhaps now it is apparent that I was wrestling with the early stages of some sort of obsessive-compulsive disorder. I would surprise myself at times with my own gruesome thoughts, and with the way they intruded into otherwise pleasant moments. A day's outing to Fort Delaware State Park, located on an island in the middle of the Delaware River, meant picnicking with a church or school group. But then I chose to linger in the bare, damp dungeons and contemplate the Confederate prisoners who had starved to death in the Union's smaller, paler version of Andersonville.

Sunday mornings found me the dutiful Sunday School pupil, absorbing a lesson about the Calvinist martyr John Hus, a religious reformer and forerunner of John Calvin, burned at the stake in Germany in 1416. I let my classmates sing their thin, sad version of "Jesus Loves Me, This I Know," while I wondered what it would be like to be roasted alive. Sitting on a metal chair, my legs swinging slowly above the wooden floor, I imagined myself bound to the stake, my body lapped by flames, my screams of anguish piercing the air. And where, I asked, was God in all of this? "Little ones to Him belong; they are weak but He is strong."

Each year I looked forward to the week my family spent at Rehoboth Beach, but invariably on some hot, sunny afternoon, sprawled out on my father's scratchy wool army blanket on the sand, I would look out over the Atlantic Ocean and think of the fate of airplane crash victims somewhere between me and Spain—the unlucky ones who were still living when the sharks came by, the tiny pieces of their body parts eventually reduced to jelly by thousands of sea creatures, the bare bones slowly sinking to their final resting place on the ocean floor. Do you faint at the first sight of a shark's fin, circling in the water nearby? How long can you remain conscious if you are bitten in two? Then my brothers would interrupt and ask if I wanted to go up to the boardwalk and get some caramel popcorn from Dolly's Taffy.

This secret inner life represented my evil twin of sorts, for on the outside I was cheerful and outgoing. As a toddler I earned a reputation in my extended family for a modest degree of charming eccentricity by concocting not one imaginary friend but a trio of them (Gonker, Ginky, and Rah-Rah). They accompanied me on my ramblings around the pond, and I clung to them even (especially?) after my two younger brothers were born. "She don't know no strangers," my babysitter Mrs. Wilder once told my mother, expressing admiration for my gregarious personality. At school I loved to hear myself talk, and not until junior high school did I catch on to the fact that dominating classroom discussion was considered an obnoxious and unladylike thing to do.

I hated my morbid streak but I also nourished it, because it provided me with a sense of who I was in contrast to everyone else. When I thought painful thoughts, I identified myself neither as a pupil at Christiana-Salem Elementary School, nor as a Presbyterian, a Phelps, or a girl.

At the same time I enjoyed the things that other kids my age did. Sitting in front of the television, I was a most undiscriminating viewer, sopping up the exploits of "Ramar of the Jungle" and "Mighty Mouse" on Saturday mornings, reveling in the antics of Jackie Gleason and Audrey Meadows on Saturday night, and following the adventures of Lassie right after marveling at the Hungarian jugglers on the Sunday night *Ed Sullivan Show*. Weekday late afternoons found me glued to the set, a loyal fan of Sally Starr and Willie the Worm (Philadelphia regional favorites), Howdy Doody and later the Mouseketeers. After dinner I watched TV families like the Nelsons and the Cleavers, but I was skeptical: These parents and children, husbands and wives, brothers and sisters all seemed to spend so much time *talking* to one another. Other shows transported me to equally strange worlds. Bishop Sheen ("Life is Worth Living") was the first Catholic clergyman I ever saw (in this case, live from a TV studio).

Movies were such a luxury that I savored every minute of each one I saw, though the poisoned-apple witch of *Snow White* and the gun leveled at Old Yeller's head left me with images that disturbed my sleep for weeks. And too, by the time I was nine or ten I came to favor historical fiction as long as there was some female character at the center. She need not be headstrong and brash—meek and pathetic would do just as well, as long as the story was interesting. So I devoured *Jane Eyre, Gone with the Wind, Lorna Doone,* and *Little Women*.

These novels reinforced my already wildly inflated view of romantic love. Surely, I thought, to fall in love with a handsome man was the great end-all and be-all of (female) existence. In this regard, the relationship between my mother and father served as both an inspiration to me and as a source of considerable resentment and frustration. While they strolled along the pungent creosote-smelling boardwalk at Rehoboth, past the shell shops and candy-cotton stands and down to the Henlopen Hotel and back again, hand in hand, I walked on in front of them, sullen in my loneliness. While they giggled and kissed during a late-afternoon summer dip in the pond, I sat on the shoreline and averted my eyes at such a disgusting spectacle. But mostly I loved to dream daydreams while sitting under the dining room table and listening to LP soundtrack recordings of *My Fair Lady, South Pacific,* and *Gigi.*

I had a hungry heart. However, winning the love of the dashing prince, or aloof professor, would seem to mandate a wistful kind of beauty on the part of the beloved, and in the looks department I fully understood that I fell very short. Although I stopped growing at age twelve and topped out at a little over five feet, during my elementary-school years I was consistently one of the tallest in my grade.

To begin with, I found it difficult to grow out of tomboyhood. One Sunday afternoon when my Jones grandmother was visiting our house, she was standing by the backyard swing set while I was hanging upside down from a sidebar. I hated the fact I had to wear a skirt to school everyday and so could not engage in this delightful activity with my friends during recess.

"Didn't you ever wish you were a boy?" Even as I asked the question I cringed, anticipating her response.

"Never," she said firmly. "Why would you ever think about such a foolish thing?" Out of seven grandchildren, I was her only grand-daughter, and no doubt something of a disappointment in terms of my indifference toward fashionable clothing and hair styles.

I understood, but only dimly and imperfectly, that my body shape was somehow related to what my female relatives looked like, and somehow related to what I ate. My teenaged cousins were trying to diet their way to thinness, but their mothers, my aunts, confirmed the principle of middle-class body types: A svelte figure must precede the mating ritual until that ritual culminated in a wedding. Thereafter, and especially with the appearance of children, the wife and mother might accept with equanimity the thickening thighs, waistline, and upper arms that were her glory as a comfortable matron.

Not yet of courtship age, I believed that I could indulge my appetite for food, and so I did, freely and thankfully. Each day at school during lunchtime I greedily eyed my friends' desserts—the slabs of homemade cake, the packages of Twinkies and Tasty Kake Butterscotch Krimpets—yearning to fill the hole in my stomach left by my two measly Oreo cookies. And so walking home from school I would stop at Baldwin's store for a NeHi orange soda and a Milky Way candy bar. By the time I got to my grandmother's house I was ready to paw through her candy dish in search of Mister Goodbars and Hershey Kisses. When I got home I might fix myself a glass of chocolate milk and a peanut butter and jelly sandwich, a little something to tide me over before dinner a couple of hours later.

My shape also reflected the contents of our kitchen. In general, the family diet bespoke less New England tradition and more 1950s convenience. Evening dinners consisted of frozen fish sticks and chicken croquettes, canned baked beans and canned peas (the added salt made this last item preferable over the fresh stuff picked from the garden)—in other words, things that needed to be defrosted, or pried out of a can, or freed of plastic wrapping. Main courses flowed as predictably as the days of the week: hot dogs, hamburgers, chicken, steak, and pork chops. I particularly appreciated the breakfast my father prepared every Sunday morning: fried eggs, bacon, sausage, and toast. My parents, and my mother especially, refrained from fussing over food. The goal was to get it out of the refrigerator or freezer and onto the table with a minimum of time and effort. We remained oblivious to edibles that had even a faintly exotic ring to them—eggplants, artichokes, avocados, romaine lettuce—and we accustomed ourselves to a limited repertoire of dishes that reminded us that food was to be consumed and not marveled over or experimented with. An open cookbook graced the kitchen counters only when it came time to prepare a dessert for a special occasion.

Because my father had grown up poor, subsisting on a diet of beans and rice, and because he had served for three and a half long years in the army eating mostly macaroni and Spam, he insisted that a slab of real meat be the centerpiece of the evening meal. Roast beef, chicken, or pork served as a measure of his success in the world. He believed that the good life consisted of a highball before dinner, a thick chunk of marbled steak during the meal, and a half pack of cigarettes afterwards. Once in a while, in a break with her own family's conventions, my mother might enjoy a small glass of Southern Comfort whiskey before dinner, and she might languidly smoke a single Marlboro afterwards. It was my father though who set the standards we followed at mealtime.

A 1957 photo taken of me, together with my two brothers, shows a chubby, round-faced little girl decked out in a sailor dress, my straight hair fastened in place with barrettes. I am peering out from behind Coke-bottle glasses (Four Eyes! Four Eyes!).

What this picture does not reveal is that fact that (I blush to admit it) I was a real slob, my person and my immediate surroundings in constant disarray. My bedroom was always messy, an elephant's grave-yard littered with schoolwork, dirty clothes, and pond collectibles (acorns, pebbles, leaf specimens). Many days I presented to the world a most unkempt appearance, to put it mildly, trotting off to school with the hem coming out of my skirt, buttons missing from my blouse and shoes scuffed to complement my bloody knees. On the other hand, I came by this apparent negligence naturally. The shock-ing condition of our kitchen counters testified to the fact that, as a family, we considered tidiness to be only a minor virtue. When visitors were expected, we straightened the stacks of magazines and moved piles of clutter into drawers.

More to the point, I lacked the compact, sleek neatness of older girls I admired—the lovely, wasp-waisted dance partners on *American Bandstand;* the multi-talented Mouseketeers like Darlene and An-nette; Hayley Mills, the very blonde *Pollyanna* movie star; and the serious skaters at the Merry Land Roller Rink who wore short skirts that showed their skinny legs. I wore dungarees and a plaid shirt that accentuated my lumpy shape.

For me, lessons in fashion, like lessons in the preparation and consumption of food, were for the most part subtle and indirect. My mother offered me few guidelines. She did feel strongly that the appropriate school uniform consisted of a white blouse with a pat-terned skirt of some kind. Stripes should never be combined with flowers, nor should polka dots ever be found in the vicinity of plaids. Under no circumstances was a red anything to be worn with a pink anything else. Black in any form (with the exception of patent leather Sunday School shoes) should not adorn the body of a little girl.

My straight, thin hair was the heaviest cross to bear. It stubbornly resisted all the fierce efforts that both my mother and I made to control and shape it. I endured hundreds of sleepless nights, my head flopping from side to side in a vain attempt to keep the bobby pins from digging into my scalp. A home permanent left my hair frizzy and flyaway for a week, then passable for a couple of more, then limp and scraggly for two more after that. Some of my Phelps cousins had beautiful strawberry red hair, and others red hair the color of bricks. Some of them possessed naturally curly or wavy locks, but I had to contend with mousy brown hair that looked matted and greasy if I went a day without washing it. Before I was twelve I had tried any number of styles (though I use the term loosely)—ponytails, braids, too short, too long. The floor of my bedroom was littered with old cans of hairspray, barrettes (they could be attached to the sides or the top of my head or to the nape of my neck), headbands (they fell forward over my nose), rubber bands, ribbons—all emblems of my shame and frustration.

My mother's help in these matters went only so far because she directed her energies toward her writing and not toward hectoring me about my physical appearance. Admirably, she lacked all interest in lavishing time, money, and energy into transforming her hopelessly ragamuffinish daughter into a debutante look-alike. While her children were little she managed to find sporadic opportunities to sit down at the typewriter—when she wrote her "Christiana Calling" column for the Newark weekly newspaper, when she covered evening school-board meetings in Newport, Stanton, and Middletown for the larger Wilmington daily, the *News Journal,* and when she helped my father prepare the reports that were his stock-in-trade as an officer of the church and as a member of the Christiana school board. I was not very old when she told me that the most important skill I could possess in life was the ability to put together a good sentence.

Despite her love of writing and literature, as a married woman she had followed her heart and labored full-time for her family. She worked as a secretary for DuPont (at the Wilmington Experimental Station) until I arrived in 1948. Thereafter, with the exception of periodic stints as a substitute teacher at local elementary schools, she stayed home. She embraced domesticity eagerly and unconditionally, happy to enjoy the normal family life that she had at one time (during the war) feared would be denied her forever. She always took pleasure in the mundane routines of a quiet household, and she inspired her children to do the same.

Put simply, then, my mother was a good homemaker but an indifferent housekeeper. Years later she would look back fondly on the drudgery that had consumed the large family she had grown up in. However, it was probably the social aspects of that work carried out together with her mother and five older sisters who were still at home then, and not the labor itself that provided the warm memories. I doubt her own mother would have thought of housework in terms of the good times it afforded.

A case in point was the chore of doing the laundry. My mother later recounted the routine in detail as it was performed in the old Webber house in the 1920s:

Washdays at our house were something else. All available children were pressed into service for the operation, which took a whole day. In warm weather it could be done on the large back porch, but most of the time the large, homemade "washbench" with its two big metal tubs, the old wooden washing machine and attendant piles of laundry dominated the kitchen, large as it was.

First Mother would sort the laundry into three large piles: "whites"—"coloreds"—and "darks." White sheets, pillowcases, towels, cotton underwear, handkerchiefs (everyone carried a clean one every day)—the first pile—were placed in a large metal clothes boiler on the kitchen range to be boiled in a strong soap solution. When Mother deemed them clean enough, they would be removed by the perilous procedure of winding them around a long, two-pronged stout wooden "clothes stick," draining for a minute over the boiler, and then plunging them into the hand-cranked washing machine for further treatment. When we children had turned the crank long enough to satisfy Mother, the clothes were put though hand-operated wringers into two rinse tubs, the second of which was liberally supplied with a liquid bluing concentrate to keep white cottons from yellowing. Colored clothes of course were not boiled, but went through the wash and two rinse tubs.

In addition, most heavily soiled clothes—work and play trousers, socks, hand towels—were always scrubbed on a hand scrubbing board. And many cotton articles—shirts, blouses, the many aprons, some dresses—were hand starched.

Dryers were of course undreamed of. The laundry was pinned to heavy wire lines that ran the length of our back yard. On fine days the process could be speeded by spreading some towels and other small flat pieces on the grass to be further bleached by the sun. . . .

Ironing accounted for yet another full day of work each week. Two of three heavy flatirons were heated on the coal range; a removable handle permitted exchanging a cooling iron for a hot one from the stove. Except for knit garments, everything was ironed, and in addition linen and starched articles had to be hand-dampened first. Contrasted with the present days of electric appliances and miracle fabrics, what a prodigious percentage of a homemaker's time was spent on the family laundry![1]

This fulsome description must be juxtaposed to my mother's own laundering activities once she became a wife and mother, for her slow-moving and resistant daughter was of little help when it came to collecting, sorting, and washing the clothes; hanging them out to dry (or later, putting them in and removing them from the electric dryer); folding them and putting them away. Assigned a predictable round of chores, whether setting the table for dinner, changing the sheets on my bed periodically, cleaning the upstairs bathroom on Saturday, scrubbing the kitchen floor when it got unbearably sticky, I could never have imagined a time in the future when I would write about these tasks with fondness or nostalgia. I still can't, and don't.

Thirty years after she delighted in laundry day as a little girl, my mother, in an effort to lessen the burdens of her own housework, eagerly embraced technological innovations of all kinds. Nevertheless, at times the consequences were unintended, if not downright perverse. Consider the yellow mangle commercial clothes iron that she received as a hand-me-down from her mother, a huge cylinder that filled half of a small room on the second floor of our house. On a weekday afternoon, she would sit in a straight-backed chair furiously pumping the knee brake, working her way through a huge basket of laundry. I marveled at her dexterity in using such an unwieldy contraption to press shirts and blouses, but I also suspected that she would not have bothered pressing sheets and pillowcases in the first place had she been using a small conventional iron. The mangle was a tyrant.

Had I had been more attentive, I would have realized that my own presumed future was inscribed in certain familiar spaces in the homes of my parents and my Phelps grandmother. On an early fall day in my mother's kitchen I could stand among the sparkling Mason jars and observe the bounty they were prepared to receive—grapes picked from my grandmother's backyard, pressed into pulp; applesauce boiling on the stove; mounds of corn cut from the cob; piles of fresh green beans; and baskets of peaches, tomatoes, and green peppers. In our upstairs back room stood those two formidable pieces of technology, the mangle and the sewing machine, awaiting my mother's deft touch. In our basement were a washtub, electric clothes washer and dryer, a commercial-sized freezer big enough to handle slabs of frozen meat (from my uncle's cows), and pantry shelves stocked with homemade and store-bought canned goods. (In the event of a nuclear war we would at least eat enough and wear clean clothes.)

Unlike my Jones grandmother, who never deigned to make any-thing out of cloth and thread, the Phelpses were skilled in all manner of needlework. My mother was a truly talented seamstress. Armed only with a pair of pinking shears, a box of pins and a tape measure, over the course of a couple of days she could transform a bolt of floral-patterned fabric into a snug-fitting sofa slipcover, with arms, back, and seat outlined in colorful piping. She made most of my clothes and some of my brothers' clothes as well. On any particular day in the late 1950s all three of us might be spotted wearing identi-cal pink, blue, and green short-sleeved plaid shirts.

My grandmother's living room was adorned with the handiwork of my aunts—on the lamp tables, doilies made of delicate tatting; on an easy chair, a homemade slipcover; over the back of the sofa, a colorful crocheted afghan; and above the mantel, the place of honor, a huge, intricate rendition of the clipper ship *The Flying Cloud,* in needle-point, the fruit of my unmarried aunt's labor. These material trap-pings of domesticity beckoned to me but I failed to heed their call. I suspect that I was the first Phelps woman in many generations who never learned to knit.

My real laboratory for what we today call female gender roles was my mother's summertime household, where I could observe first-hand the rhythms and responsibilities of married life. With the ex-ception of a week in summer Bible School, and a day here or there when I was charged with the hot, hateful task of picking weeds in my father's garden, no structured activity marred my long weeks of vaca-tion. Mornings my mother busied herself with a predictable round of laundering and ironing, and a phone conversation or two with her sisters. The day was punctuated by lunchtime, a ritual that consisted of egg salad sandwiches consumed in front of the television set, which was tuned to the soap opera *As the World Turns.* About this time my father would call from his office to check in with my mother, who would give him the day's news and list the pieces of mail that had arrived. Afternoons were taken up by errands to the grocery store in Ogletown, the fabric store in Newark, J.C. Penney in Newport, or, if we were lucky, Wilmington Dry Goods "in town." This, then, was the everyday life of a married Phelps—blessedly routine, comfortably secure, revealing of a fate (that certainly seemed to me) worth embracing.

When I was ten I plunged headlong into formal preparation for this life by becoming a charter member of the Greenleaf 4-H Club, which drew upon the rural and working-class environs of Newark. Sponsored by the Agricultural Extension division at the University of Delaware, the 4-H movement achieved its purest form downstate, where the farmers and farmwives of tomorrow raised their own cows and sheep, groomed their own horses, and drove the tractors that harvested their own fields of corn. In suburban New Castle County, we could not aspire to this level of agricultural productivity, of course, and so contented ourselves (the girls at least) with cooking corn muffins, sewing skirts and aprons, and growing a few tomatoes here and there.

My involvement in 4-H (the four H's of Head, Heart, Health and Hands) represented both the beginning and the end of my commitment to meaningful club activity of any kind. (I was briefly a member of the local Brownie Troop, but as far as I can tell I joined primarily so that I could wear the uniform of a light brown dress and dark brown beanie, a privilege soon overshadowed by the unpleasant duty of selling Girl Scout cookies door-to-door in Christiana.) 4-H was an odd blend of the domestic arts overlaid with cutthroat competition. We were preparing ourselves to be future homemakers, but we learned that such an endeavor necessarily set us one against the other, cook against cook, seamstress against seamstress. All paths led to Ag Hall at the University, where members of the county clubs would model their clothing or prepare a dish, all under the watchful eyes of judges. A lucky few of the contestants then took their sewing or cooking show on the road, to the state fair, held downstate (in Harrington) each July. And so we all joined together, as individuals, in the blue-ribbon chase.

I did enjoy competing at school, but I never developed the killer instinct so necessary to succeed in 4-H. I was known to omit baking soda from the recipe for chocolate chip cookies. I was known to sit hunched over, my face red-hot with rage, ripping out one misplaced seam after another, time and again, on the most simple of garments. My clothes pattern of choice was the apron, for it had no encumbrances that required specialized skills—no buttonholes, zippers, sleeves, plackets, interfacing or cuffs. I did manage to reach the state finals twice—once with a demonstration called "How to Make a Pocket," and once with a dinner dish called (I have no idea why) "Chicken for a Summer Day," a thick, greasy concoction with almonds thrown in the mix. Even these modest activities thrust me into the maelstrom of 4-H politics, with charges and countercharges circulating before and after the events in question: one judge favored contestants from Kent County, another judge cared less about the product in question and more about the neat and ladylike appearance of the contestant (in which case, of course, I was sunk).

My defining moment as a 4-H competitor came during a demonstration, "How to Prepare a Tossed Salad," one Saturday afternoon in a basement room of Ag Hall. I was twelve, old enough to know that I should be very nervous. I helped my mother make salads all the time, but it struck me as exceedingly unnatural to have to prepare any kind of food while a stranger was hovering over me, monitoring my every move, checklist on clipboard in hand. At home that morning, I had stood in the kitchen and carefully packed a brown paper grocery bag with all the food and equipment I would need for my upcoming ordeal. Mindful of the havoc that a dull knife could wreak on a tomato—the blade smooshing rather than cutting the tough skin, the seeds and the insides splattering all over everything—at the last minute I threw my mother's mean little razor-sharp paring knife into the bulging grocery bag. The rest of the story is so predictable it hardly merits retelling.

After waiting an eternity for my turn, sitting through a parade of girls icing cakes, making piecrusts, and preparing French toast, I was called to the front of the room. I placed my ingredients on the large demonstration table, which had a huge mirror positioned over it, so that the judge could keep an eye on my hands. I managed to shred the lettuce and chop the cucumbers in a competent way before turning my attention to the tomato. The knife slid cleanly through not only its skin, but through mine as well, and my thumb began to bleed profusely on top of the greens I had assembled so carefully in the bowl below. Muttering to myself, I tried to remain calm as I reached for a piece of paper towel that might staunch the flow of blood so that I could get on with the business at hand. Surprisingly, the judge approached the table and discreetly passed me a Band-Aid, but my fingers were wet and slippery and it would not adhere. I threw in the rest of the ingredients and called it a day, taking my seat at the back of the room, humiliated. At the end of the afternoon, the judge, in her humanity, awarded me a second-place red ribbon—for my composure, I suppose, because I had managed not to cry. The experience confirmed in my mind what I already knew—that I was a failure, a fraud, when it came to the most simpleminded of tasks carried out within the confines of the kitchen.

Gradually I fell from grace as a 4-H'er. The older I got, the less focus and energy I was able to muster in the competitive realm of homemaking politics. Secretly I cherished failure (modest as it was), simply because it reinforced my own sense of myself as an outsider in yet another world, this one domestic.

In 1960, when I was twelve, I began to abandon Christiana. As a family we would always live there, but as an adolescent I gradually turned my back on the town, eager to look and live away from it. Just a few miles away, Ogletown was an unlikely destination for an increasingly restless spirit; by 1960 the old settlement, even less substantial than Christiana, had been consumed by tract housing developments with the names of Brookside, Chestnut Hill Estates, Robscott Manor, Todd Estates. Ogletown Junior High School was shaped like a giant letter E, with each of three wings housing ten homerooms of grades seven through nine—nearly one thousand seventh, eighth and ninth graders under the same roof. If elementary school had represented a compact, lively little theater, then junior high was a gigantic movie set—bigger, flashier, with a more diverse cast of even more glamorous characters. In this new school, I encountered archetypes that I had never dreamed of, including the Brain, a human slide rule; the Loose Girl, who inspired a mixture of contempt and envy in the rest of us (we all failed to appreciate the relative significance of the Loose Boy at the same time); the Jock (male or female) who actually knew how to wield a field-hockey stick or handle a basketball with some precision.

The Ogletown teachers were not only fascinating in their own right, but also at least some of them were men. And so in the seventh grade I fell in love with a kind of person whom I had never met before—Mr. Rothman, my science teacher, dark, intense, good-looking, Jewish. I met kids from the suburbs of Newark (some of them the children of college professors) and learned what a Villager sweater was and why I should desire one. I began to care what I looked like before I ran out of the house to catch the bus every morning. Seventh grade marked the first time I attended a school dance, visited someone who lived in a split-level house, played my clarinet with members of a band, and learned how to put my hair up with (though not necessarily sleep in) brush rollers. The social scene had shifted from the front porch of Baldwin's store to the Ogletown Junior High Cafeteria. I was in the process of leaving home.

Nevertheless, this process was an uneven one. When I was twelve I underwent a number of separate rites of passage. In the spring I formally joined the Christiana Presbyterian Church, and I remember feeling gratified to formalize a long-standing connection with this most significant of Phelps institutions. In the summer, for my twelfth birthday my father presented me with a .22 rifle, a rural Delaware coming-of-age gift for a firstborn (girl or boy). I soon learned that I could compete with my Jones cousins when it came to shooting tin cans for target practice down at the dump behind our house. My father was proud of me, but it was a little too late to devote myself to either marksmanship or hunting. That Thanksgiving, he suggested that we go hunting together for rabbits in the morning, after church and before dinner, a kind of father-daughter bonding ritual. I enjoyed the walk in the woods but guns scared me, and I worried about inflicting harm on myself or on him. Later in the day I gave thanks that we had all safely survived the morning—my father, the beasts of the fields and the forests, and me.

A couple of days later I got my period. This was an obvious nuisance, but my older, well-put-together cousin (whose boxes of sanitary napkins still sat unopened on the shelf of her bedroom closet) was envious, providing me with some small measure of satisfaction.

By this time my oldest cousins had already staked out careers for themselves, and I began to ponder the problem of finding something that I was good at. In 1960 my oldest Jones cousin was in college, preparing for veterinary school, and the two oldest Phelps cousins, male and female, were an Air Force pilot and a nurse, respectively. Thereafter, the three remaining Joneses would become a park ranger, electrician and farrier (blacksmith), while the Phelpses would take up social work, nursing (three altogether), office administration, and tractor-trailer truck driving. Gradually, out of the total of eleven cousins, five would remain in Delaware and the rest (including my brothers and I) would move out of state. Sunday afternoon gatherings, their size and their emotional significance for me, diminished gradually over time.

When I was in seventh grade my beloved Phelps grandmother died. In keeping with the view that funerals were inappropriate occasions for children, neither my brothers nor I attended the service. Yet I needed no ritual to understand that her death marked the definitive end of my childhood.

My mother and aunts spent the weeks after her death and on into the spring sorting through a treasure trove in the attic of her house. One day I came home from school and found a huge bonfire roaring in the backyard. Clothes, furniture, and family memorabilia of various kinds were consigned to the flames—it was the time just before rural Protestants would come to feel beleaguered by a rising chorus of "ethnics," the time before preserving family history assumed the significance of a political act.

Within a few months my Phelps uncle and his family had relocated from Newport to the white frame house next to ours, thus helping to perpetuate the Phelps name and presence in Christiana. My unmarried aunt now left home for the first time, moved to an apartment in Wilmington, and later fulfilled a lifelong dream by going to Vietnam as a Bible translator and missionary. My uncle's family retained their membership in the large, inner city West Presbyterian Church in Wilmington and from that vantage point they began to diverge perceptibly from the Christiana-based Phelpses on matters related to the civil rights movement. Conventional extended-family wisdom held that "too much was happening too quickly" and that "it was not possible to legislate changes in people's hearts and minds." In contrast, my uncle's family knew African Americans as friends and as coreligionists, and understood better than we the larger forces that were transforming Wilmington in particular, and all of New Castle County.

For example, bulldozers were beginning to bisect Wilmington's black neighborhood to make way for the highway that would become Interstate 95, and white people were leaving the city, fleeing from its newly integrated schools. Over the next decade, the percentage of blacks in the city's population would increase from 25 to 43 percent, a trend that accelerated in the last quarter of the twentieth century. Once a southern city, Wilmington was in the process of becoming northern, like Detroit or Cleveland.

Spotlighting only the South, though, the evening news carried footage of bloody Freedom Riders and stoic lunch-counter demonstrators. I was aware that a great struggle was underway somewhere in the country, but not in Christiana.

Throughout my career I have resisted the notion that history is a form of autobiography. Despite the prevalence of identity politics these days, no social group has a claim on a particular topic or field of scholarship, historical or otherwise. And yet I suppose a case could be made for the idea that, in certain respects at least, I have spent much of my adult life writing about Christiana, if rather obliquely, exploring the dynamics of social relations that I first observed on a modest scale in the 1950s, in my hometown.

It is also possible that my own historical research amounts to little more than a desperate attempt to atone for my close association with mid-twentieth century Delaware, which, in the words of one scholar, "functioned as a fossilized racist encampment on the traditionally white-supremacist Eastern Shore peninsula."[2] Delaware had spawned a peculiar form of Jim Crow. Mississippi, with its long history of staple-crop agriculture, at least possessed a clear-cut economic rationale for black subordination—the exploitation of large numbers of field hands over the generations. Yet Delaware's institutionalized prejudice seemed almost free-floating, detached from any larger economic purpose. The state's peculiar power structure, based on an unholy alliance between upstate corporate money (centered in Wilmington) and downstate rural interests (dispersed through Kent and Sussex Counties) had produced an intriguing hybrid, blending the worst of the Deep South's *de jure* discrimination with the worst of the North's *de facto* hypocrisy. To be a native daughter of such a place would seem to require some explanation, some self-justification, preferably in the form of a life's work.

Not until I graduated from high school and entered the University of Delaware did I strike out on my own and began to view the world in decidedly un-Phelps-like ways. By this time, I had learned about the war in Vietnam and about the civil-rights movement in the South. The distance separating a complacent Christiana from a more restless Newark (site of the university, which I entered in 1966) seemed much greater than five miles. Back home, the Sunday-morning sermons delivered at the Christiana Presbyterian Church became more overtly political, and literally conservative in the sense they offered explicit denunciations of civil-rights activists, welfare mothers, and antiwar protesters. Subsequently I abandoned the faith of my forebears. The message of universal brotherly love had become twisted into a weekly, one-hour screed against godless Communism and its vicious offspring, radicals of different stripes and darker skin colors.

Lacking much in the way of direction in college, I bounced from one field of concentration to another. As a sophomore I was majoring in German, preparing for a career as a high school language teacher. By the next year I had switched to sociology, trying to understand a world engulfed in political violence, rocked by assassinations and urban civil rebellions. Within a year I had decided to pick up yet one more set of change-of-major forms at the Office of the Registrar; unable to focus on any one topic for more than a course or two, I became an American Studies major so I would not have to major in anything at all.

In my final two years at Delaware I discovered an intellectual niche, if not a discipline to go with it. For the most part I found history classes to be dull and narrow. I maintained a studied indifference toward European intrigue and the kings, princes, popes and prime ministers who were the stock figures in textbooks. Even American intellectual and political history struck me as lacking in the drama of the time I was living in. For this reason, my first class in African American history came as something of a revelation. No one at Delaware was prepared to teach the subject in the late 1960s, so the History Department imported Professor Thomas Cripps, a faculty member at Morgan State College (now University) in Baltimore, and an authority on African Americans in film, to offer the survey. This single course opened up a whole new world for me. It encouraged me to think more broadly about history, and to challenge conventional definitions of work, achievement, progress.

During my senior year I helped to coordinate the University of Delaware's quintessential 1960s liberal social-action project, which sent undergraduate college students into Wilmington's inner-city neighborhoods every Saturday afternoon. Linked to the project was a course in urban sociology offered Wednesday nights. Saturdays I found myself back at church, but now in one of the several inner-city Presbyterian churches that provided space for our program, and for the first time in my life this space was drained of religious meaning, even as it was infused with social purpose.

This effort was premised on the dubious assumption that contact between middle-class white college students and poor black kids would help to address some of the fundamental structural inequalities in the United States at the time. Exploring the historical roots of the relation between white teachers and black pupils, I wrote a senior thesis on a group of Quaker philanthropists who had established schools for African American children in Delaware soon after the end of the Civil War. The group they founded, the Delaware Association for the Moral Improvement and Education of the Colored People, had sent one of its pioneer volunteer teachers to Christiana, where she began a small school that formed the antecedent to 111-C. This study, completed under the expert direction of Professor John Munroe, the dean of Delaware history, introduced me to the joys of primary research.

By the time I was ready to graduate from college in 1970, I realized that I was unprepared for a specific job of any kind, and further, that I had no interest in leaving a newfound life of study and intellectual engagement to become a productive member of society. So I applied to and was accepted in a new graduate program sponsored by the Ford Foundation through the Educational Policy Studies Department at the University of Wisconsin, Madison. The purpose of the program was to train administrators for inner-city public school systems. My application essay focused on the property tax and the unequal funding of public schooling throughout the state of Delaware. (I had worked in the office of the Governor's Special Assistant for Urban Affairs the summer after my junior year.)

It soon became apparent to me that a career in school administration was not my calling; I lacked interest in and patience for bureaucracies and budgets. And so within a year of my arrival in Madison I transferred to the History Department and embarked on a course of study that allowed me to pursue my fascination with the teachers I had studied for my senior thesis at college. The result was a dissertation (and then a book)[3] on the teachers who went south to Georgia after the Civil War, most of them the young, unmarried daughters of New England farmers, clergymen, and craftsmen. The group I studied was sponsored by the American Missionary Association, the missionary arm of the Presbyterian and Congregational churches.

The teachers' story was a familiar one to me. These idealistic, well-educated white women scorned the routines associated with domestic service and school teaching, and sought a "wider field of usefulness" during this time of glorious struggle. To complete the heroic work of their brothers and fathers, men who had subdued the rebels and freed the slaves with rifle and bayonet, the teachers would invade the South with "light and love." I well understood the teachers' indignation over the system of bondage, their sense of adventure, and especially their naive faith in the power of good intentions to right historic wrongs.

What was not familiar to me in this history saga was the political thrust of African American culture as created and sustained by the freedpeople of Georgia immediately after the war. Emblematic of that culture was the Savannah Education Association, a group founded by leading black clergymen and politicians soon after Sherman's troops liberated the city in December of 1864. The determination of the SEA to control the education of the city's African American children and adults—to transform the old slave market into classrooms, to hire teachers and sponsor fund-raisers—met with opposition from the northern missionaries and their allies, agents of the United States Freedmen's Bureau and officers of the Union army. To these northern whites, schooling was a form of largesse bestowed upon the former slaves; but to the freed men and women of Georgia, schooling took the form of a community, as well as an individual, endeavor, one that bespoke their status as free people and citizens as well as responsible parents. Within a couple of years of its founding, however, the SEA had collapsed, unable to raise enough money to sustain itself, and the northerners had sanctimoniously, even gleefully, assumed control over the fledgling school system of Savannah.

The white schoolteachers' stubborn belief in the transcendent significance of hard work and literacy offered me a lesson in processes of historical change. While the young women preached punctuality (in the fields), thrift, and sobriety, the freedpeople were denied access to the resources that would have enabled them to become independent of former slaveholders—land, cash, credit. As I followed the teachers' reports from the field, hundreds of letters sent from 1865 to 1873, I began to see the larger picture that most of them could not or would not. Only the handful who remained in the state for more than a few years comprehended the matrix of political and economic factors that would eventually return power to white supremacists.

Certainly the postbellum southern classroom of squirming, eager "abcedarians" was a battleground of sorts, just as Reconstruction itself was an extension of the Civil War. After 1865, however, northern and southern whites joined forces in promoting the neoslavery system of sharecropping. In the late 1860s, southern whites terrorized African American voters, teachers, and political leaders, and before too long white northerners lost interest in all matters related to the rights (human as well as civil) of African Americans. In charting the development of postwar southern society, I discovered that individual strivings counted for less than the political and economic structures created by groups of people motivated by power and its corollary, racial prejudice.

These issues drew me to new historical scholarship in the field of African American history—works such as John Blassingame's *The Slave Community: Plantation Life in the Antebellum South* (1972); Eugene Genovese's *Roll, Jordan, Roll: The World the Slaves Made* (1976); and Herbert G. Gutman's *The Black Family in Slavery and Freedom, 1750–1925* (1976). In graduate school I also learned about a new political movement consisting of a group I had never thought much about in any systematic way—women. Madison in the early 1970s was a good place and time to have one's consciousness raised, simply because no one was in the mood to lavish sympathy on middle-class white girls. Only groups that demonstrated revolutionary potential seemed worthy of respect—the anti-racist, industrial saboteurs who formed the Dodge Revolutionary Movement in Detroit; the Black Panthers, a group of Black-Power militants; the insurgent farmworkers of Cesar Chavez's La Raza; and of course the peasant guerillas of postcolonial Vietnam, the Viet Cong.

My comrades in graduate school were writing their dissertations on the Industrial Workers of the World in World War I–era Mexican oil fields; Irish immigrants to Chicago in the late nineteenth century; the Lawrence, Massachusetts, textile workers' strike of 1912; and California agricultural laborers. Rather apologetically, I began to develop an interest in women's history. Yet I never embraced a brand feminism that was all-consuming, that is, focused narrowly on women to the exclusion of other groups barred from the rights and privileges of white men of "property and standing."

In 1985 I finished a book on the history of African American women and the tension between the labor demanded of them by whites and the duties they performed for their own families and communities.[4] That book had its origins in a women's history survey course I developed at Wellesley College. As a newly minted Ph.D. and a beginning assistant professor, I was surprised that my students held such misguided notions of work—that they believed paid employment was an intrinsically liberating activity—and that they knew so little about African American history in general.

While compiling census data on late nineteenth-century southern Cotton Belt households as part of that project, I was struck by the similarities in household structure between African American and white families. These families organized their productive energies in the same way, they demonstrated similar demographic patterns (large numbers of children within two-parent households), and they remained poor, enmeshed in the brutal systems of peonage, share-cropping, and tenancy. And so in my next book I explored the history of poverty among blacks and whites after the Civil War, and traced southern migrants into the Midwest after 1916 or so.[5] In this work I encountered some groups whose work histories evoked 1950s Delaware—men and women migrants from Appalachia who had moved north to work in auto factories, and migrant laborers who went "on the season" up the East Coast each summer and fall, follow-ing the harvest.

I found that poor whites retained significant advantages over their black counterparts. Although members of both groups lacked much in the way of "industrial discipline" or formal education, and al-though both adhered to Protestant fundamentalist beliefs and rear-ed large families, the whites benefited from racially discriminatory hiring and residential policies. White men had access to semiskilled jobs and the opportunity to ascend internal ladders of mobility in factories and other work sites. Their families enjoyed the kind of residential mobility that allowed them to move wherever their in-clination and household income would take them. In contrast, black workers were forced to stay on the lowest rung of the work ladder, confined to menial, low-paying jobs regardless of their skills or ambi-tion, and they were limited to center-city neighborhoods where the public schools received disproportionately low levels of funding and where large numbers of poor people were concentrated.

In developing the idea of racial ideology as a form of political strategy deployed by whites, I drew upon what is arguably the most significant work of scholarship in the field of American history—Edmund Morgan's *American Slavery, American Freedom: The Ordeal of Colonial Virginia*. Morgan explores contingencies that spawned ide-ologies of racial difference as they emerged during the colonial period of American history. Rather than revealing innate prejudices, these ideologies expressed the anxieties of specific groups of people at specific times. Even after the colonial period, the forms and func-tions of racial prejudice remained in flux, shaped by any number of factors, including military defense considerations, immigration, par-tisan politics, territorial growth, and technological innovation. From

Morgan I learned not to take prejudice for granted, but to explore precise regional and national configurations of power and wealth in order to answer the question: Given historical change, who wins and who loses, and why?

My interest in the complex mechanisms by which different groups of people were assigned to, or sought, different kinds of jobs, led to another project, this one focusing on the so-called racial division of labor throughout American history.[6] In fact no one fixed set of beliefs or laws held sway over the structure of the labor market. Rather, the prejudices that limited black people to certain kinds of jobs were fluid, and at times contradictory. Thus, during the antebellum period, members of the white laboring classes in the North could charge blacks with predatory behavior in the workplace—supposedly, black men's drive for good jobs would deprive white men of their livelihood and reduce white families to "beggary." Simultaneously these same white men claimed that blacks were shiftless, lazy, a drain on the public treasury. In the late twentieth century, this apparent contradiction still persisted, when demagogic whites decried blacks' efforts to crack formerly all-white schools and jobs, and at the same time condemned blacks en masse as slackers dependent on the public dole. The low-income women (especially minority women) who chose to care for their children at home full-time, as my mother had done in the 1950s, found little respect among either their well-to-do neighbors or local or federal policy makers.

Clearly, it is not possible to study any one group in complete isolation from others. The overlapping and interlocking social signifiers that characterized Christiana in the 1950s mocked my efforts to isolate gender from racial factors, religious from class factors. One way to appreciate the complexity of historical change, and the complexity of social organization, is to study the division of labor, which constitutes the fundamental building block of any society. In a recent book I explore the idea that labor history encompasses all forms of activity that lead to the production of goods and services, whether those activities are waged or unwaged, or carried out in urban or rural areas by men, women, or children. To understand the relations among different kinds of workers, relations that were at once symbiotic and wracked with conflict, is to understand the everyday struggles of ordinary people. By investigating work we can grasp the grand sweep of American history.[7]

In the decade beginning in 1976 I became an historian, a New Englander, a wife, a Jew, and the mother of two daughters, in that order. Momentously, I fell in love with a Jewish man, a professor, and embraced his faith. Born and raised only an hour from Christiana, in the suburbs of Philadelphia, he came from a family with historical roots in Eastern Europe (Minsk, Belarus, and Riga, Latvia). I was struck by the fact that his family demonstrated a propensity to speak their minds, forcefully, on all manner of subjects. By this time I had distanced myself from my Presbyterian roots, and saw my conversion to Judaism (literally on the eve of the birth of my first daughter) as an affirmation of the future of my own new family.

In my scholarly work I had come to appreciate the values that seem peculiarly American—the willingness to move in search of a better job or a safer place to raise your children, and the willingness to follow your heart regardless of the demographic signifiers, the boxes, into which the circumstances of your birth had initially assigned you. I suppose then that there is a clear connection between what I observed in my hometown in Delaware in the 1950s and the themes I chose to write about later in my life. At the same time, I would argue that those themes—the great migrations and economic transformations of American history, the efforts of workers of all kinds to control their own productive energies—are transcendent issues and require no autobiographical context to explain or justify them.

It now seems perfectly natural that, at a certain point in my life, I would become curious to learn how Christiana had fared over the course of the last four decades of the twentieth century. And so I began by looking for answers in a classroom in my old and, as it turned out, much altered, elementary school.

Epilogue
Creek Walkers at the Millennial Crossroads

It was a dreary Friday afternoon in January at the end of the twentieth century, and anticipation of the weekend crackled through the room like an electric current. Still, the fourth graders in Ms. Lyle's class at the Albert H. Jones Elementary School were remarkably patient with the visitor from Boston who plied them all sorts of questions: Where were they were born and what did they do during summer vacation? What kinds of pets did they have at home? As it turned out, they boasted an assortment of animals not all that different from those collected by the students who had left the school many years before—dogs, rabbits, cats, fish, hamsters, and birds, with only a few hermit crabs and a stray ten-foot python to mark these as kids of the late 1990s and not 1950s. During music class, they liked to sing "Somewhere Over the Rainbow" and "We're Off to See the Wizard."

In response to the query, "What do you like to do after school?" they began reporting, one by one, that they did their homework, watched TV, rode their bikes, jumped on their pogo sticks, played baseball and basketball, practiced their musical instruments, and "went online." Candor seemed to be the order of the day: "I fight with my sister," said one girl. "I make prank calls," said a boy. Finally, one member of the class, who had waited to be called upon, announced that after school he liked to go "creek walking." The visitor stopped what she was doing, put her notebook down, and asked what he meant. Her tone was so insistent, startled almost, that the class became quiet, and all eyes turned toward the creek walker.

"I like to walk along the side of the creek, you know, to explore," he said.

"The creek? Do you mean the river? The Christina River?" she asked.

141

He gestured out the window, to the area down West Main Street, toward the stone bridge. "Yeah, the river, the creek. I like to slide down the bank and see what I can find—old stuff. I found pieces of an old trailer once."

Standing there in Mrs. Petrocelli's old classroom, I felt truly at home again, in the company of a soulmate some forty years my junior.

The eighteen white kids and ten black kids in the class were exuberant and charming, "full of beans," as my aunts might have described them. Remembering my own slovenly years in the fourth grade, they struck me as a remarkably well-groomed and tidy lot. One little girl—her hair neatly plaited in tiny braids on top of her head, her dress as fresh as the moment it had come out of the dryer, her white anklet socks neatly folded down above unscuffed shoes—told me that she hoped to become a model someday. Indeed, she looked like she had just stepped out of an ad for Gap Kids.

Members of the class were curious about earlier days at the school. I explained that when I entered first grade no black children were allowed to attend. "That was because of prejudice," one boy noted simply. Appropriately enough, they expressed horror over the evil uses to which Mrs. Petrocelli had put her blood-red pointy thumbnail (*in this very room!*) and the fact that girls were not allowed to wear shorts or pants ("Did you wear those funny '70s clothes?" someone asked me, unaware of what funny '50s clothes even looked like; I couldn't bear to tell him that I was of the *Father Knows Best* rather than *Brady Bunch* vintage.) But they seemed most intrigued by the description of the razzle-dazzle—just thinking about it literally brought a few of them out of their seats—and its weird corollary, the seeming indifference of the playground monitors to the fact that we risked life and limb every day on the gray metal monster.

The class provided a demographic profile of New Castle County in the late 1990s. At least a quarter had been born outside Delaware, with the black youngsters coming from Alabama, Virginia, and North Carolina. Their white classmates who had moved from out of state hailed from Indiana, New York, Texas, and Pennsylvania. During the summer they all visited cousins and grandparents living in these states and others—Florida, South Carolina, and Tennessee. The school and the area immediately around it have retained a southern feel, from the sound of the soft drawl of the vice principal, a native of Houston, to the aroma of savory powdermilk biscuits and fried chicken served at the Bob Evans Restaurant right up the street. One little boy with a southern accent approached me after the bell had rung and said, "I always wondered what the daughter of Albert H. Jones looked like."

The school stuck me as a blend of old and new. At the end of the day, designated eraser-clappers ran outside to finish their chores before heading home. The cursive writing chart hanging above the blackboard in Ms. Lyle's room looked like a holdover from the bad-old Petrocelli days. But the school was much bigger now: a new two-story wing helped to accommodate 634 youngsters in five grades, kindergarten through fourth, more than one-third of them African American. On the walls in the hallway hung timelines of Martin Luther King's life, individual posters drawn in crayon by the third graders (one ending in 1968 with a picture of a tiny tombstone), and the display next to the principal's office announced the theme of the month: "Exploring Many Worlds Under One Sky." Outside, the playground equipment consisted of elaborate labyrinths made out of colorful molded plastic, no doubt certified by safety specialists.

In the school newsletter, called "Keeping Up With the Joneses," I read that the first graders in Ms. Dunston's class have been learning about the Delaware Leni-Lenape Indians ("We made clay coil pots, buffalo prints, beaded necklaces and a feathered headdress"); that students practice writing through a curriculum called writers' workshop, which includes "mini-lesson, prewriting activities, rough draft, peer and teacher conferencing, editing and finally, publishing"; and that the $800 raised by a school-wide "penny project" went to help the Christiana firefighters buy a single pair of the expensive vision goggles that they had long wanted but could not afford; the price for one pair amounted to $20,000—no doubt the cost of a whole engine when I was growing up.

Almost all of the kids in the school were bused (the creek walker in Ms. Lyle's class was exceptional in that respect). Not surprisingly, then, the end of the school day appeared to consist of barely controlled chaos, with teachers and monitors communicating through walkie-talkies in order to load a dozen or so buses quickly and efficiently. Some children could look forward to—or dread, as the case might be—a bus ride of as much as twelve miles each way; these were the ones who lived in west center-city Wilmington and came in on I-95 each day. When I asked them what school they would be attending next year, I received a bewildering number of answers. In name at least Ogletown Junior High no longer exists, and instead, they would either choose or be assigned to one of several theme schools (for the gifted/talented, or for those interested in science, math, physical well-being, the Spanish language, or entrepreneurship).

The Jones school (named for my father after his death in 1995) is one of twelve kindergarten-through-fourth-grade elementary schools in the Christina School District, formed in 1980. Two years earlier the state of Delaware had found itself under a court order issued by the United States District Court in Wilmington and forced to come up with a plan to desegregate its New Castle County schools. Basically, this meant that the majority-black city of Wilmington had to be integrated with the majority-white suburbs in the northern part of the state.

The order originated in 1971 with a lawsuit filed by black parents in Wilmington who argued that the state had willfully ignored the mandate of *Brown vs. the Board,* and that the Wilmington school officials had left intact a system of segregated schools. The courts pressured the state to respond. In 1975 a variety of groups, including individual school districts, the League of Women Voters, the State Board of Education (of which my father was president), coalitions of private citizens, groups of parents of school children, and the Community Legal Aid Association all weighed in with separate plans to integrate the New Castle County schools. Finally, the state legislature created the administrative apparatus for implementing a plan, the so-called New Board, in the summer of 1976. This body consisted of two representatives each from the largest districts to be affected, Wilmington and Newark, and one representative each from the other eleven districts involved.

During the ensuing planning stage, new organizations sprang up on both sides of the issue. Against "forced busing" of any kind (and of course integration depended on busing) was a group with the misleading name Positive Action Committee (their call to resistance: "It's Time to Wake Up Folks"). In the late 1970s the committee claimed to have 10,000 members. Supporters of the court order formed the Delaware Educational Process Committee and the Delaware Committee for the School Decision. In the fall of 1978, the schools in a new, countywide single district were integrated peacefully.[1] Not long after that, this single district was divided into five new ones; besides Christina, the other four now include Colonial (surrounding New Castle), Brandywine, Red Clay, and Appoquinimink (this last covering the southern, most rural part of the county below the Chesapeake and Delaware Canal). The goal of the system was to distribute the county's black children (about 20 percent of the total) evenly throughout these newly redrawn districts.[2]

In the year 2000, Christina was the largest school district in the state, and the state's fifteenth largest employer, with 21,000 children in its schools and 2,255 full-time workers on the payroll. Among its unusual characteristics was its non-contiguous shape—the eastern part (the western section of Wilmington) was separated by several miles from the western part, an area that ran from the middle of New Castle County westward to the Maryland line. District "feeder patterns" decreed that the Wilmington kids must spend at least nine of their public-school years in the suburbs, and that the suburban kids must spend at least three of theirs in the city of Wilmington. Overall, the Jones school reflected the racial makeup of the immediate region, with 36 percent black pupils, 56.8 percent white, 4 percent Hispanic, and 2.7 percent Asian American. About one out of three of the kids came from a low-income family. The instructional staff was 95 percent female and 86 percent white.

Thirty-one children, or about 5 percent of the Jones student body, were "choice" students, meaning their parents won a place for their son or daughter at the school through a lottery. It is for this reason perhaps that both the school newsletter and the elaborate "school profile" available to visitors have a certain boosterish quality about them. From these materials I am pleased to learn that the school has placed second in the district in its writing scores on a Delaware state standardized test, and that the fourth graders placed first in their region in a recent statewide Math League competition. The official mission of the school reads as follows: "We, the Albert H. Jones Elementary School, a caring family community, teach and value our children by supporting them as individuals who progress at their own pace and in their own learning styles in a safe, positive environment."

Well, my father would have been proud. Ironically, though, the very existence of the Jones school is a measure of the turbulent times faced by the city of Wilmington, his hometown. In response to the assassination of Martin Luther King, Jr., in 1968, the black community, which represented a little more than a third of the city's population, launched a violent civil rebellion, the result of years—generations, really—of pent-up rage and frustration over a lack of economic and educational opportunities. Well into the 1960s, too many white folks, including the highest state officials, insisted on celebrating their own racist heritage. For example, in a move calculated less to restore order and more to humiliate Wilmington African Americans, Governor Charles L. Terry, Jr. called up the state's National Guard and then kept the city under military occupation, from April 1968 until January of 1969 (when his successor, Russell Peterson, withdrew the troops). White civic groups sponsored open forums entitled "What Do the Negroes Want?" apparently oblivious to the state's history. "What Do Negroes Want?" indeed, as if this question amounted to some deep, dark mystery. A superficial understanding of the state's past—distant or recent—would have provided much of the answer. White parents might have also asked themselves what *they* wanted—presumably good schools, safe neighborhoods, and decent jobs—in order better to appreciate the aspirations of the African Americans in the state.

During the 1970s, suburbanites began to shun Wilmington's downtown commercial center in favor of the new malls that were springing up outside the city limits, and in 1975 the Wilmington Medical Center, a consortium of hospitals, announced that it would be building an 800-bed facility in the suburbs. Christiana Hospital is located just a mile or so from "the Corner" today. In the early 1980s the state legislature passed the Financial Center Development Act and other banking legislation that not only spurred the growth of the state's financial services industry, but also changed the skyline of downtown Wilmington, now sprouting new glass and chrome office towers.

The conjunction of these two seemingly contradictory trends—the shriveling of the once-vital commercial district on the one hand, and the booming business community on the other—renders Wilmington a prime example of an eerie postindustrial urban landscape. Long gone are Kennards, Wilmington Dry Goods and Reynolds Restaurant. The last movie theaters closed in the early 1980s. In the place of these businesses now are community action centers and mom-and-pop stores operated by African Americans and Asian immigrants. (My mother teaches English to a Korean shopkeeper whose corner grocery, in a predominantly black and Hispanic neighborhood in northeast Wilmington, has paid for her Americanized children's college educations.) During the day, banking executives enjoy lunch in company dining rooms and then venture only as far as highrise parking lots before heading back home after work. Over the last half century, the city's population has fallen from 100,000 to 70,000 people, the majority of them black, while the suburbs remain 90 percent white.

New Castle County is a microcosm of national trends revealing of a high-tech economy undergirded by low-wage service industries.[3] Driving down I-95 from Philadelphia today, the motorist is greeted at the Delaware state line with a sign that reads, "Welcome to Delaware, Home of Tax-Free Shopping." Retail trade accounts for about 20 percent of the state's labor force, and the malls and superstore complexes in New Castle County, their wares unencumbered by sales taxes, draw customers from neighboring states. The state as a whole reaps the mixed blessings of its financial and health-care services economy. The population has grown steadily in recent years, and with 732,000 people in 1997 it is exactly twice as large as it was in 1950. The finance, insurance, and real estate component of the economy posted the fastest growth in the decade of the nineties, increasing at an average annual rate of 15 percent.

The jobs of the parents of Ms. Lyle's pupils mirrored the local and state economy. Delaware's growing health-care industry was represented by a parent employed by Principal Health Care, and one of the fathers worked at the gigantic Amazon.Com warehouse now located near the New Castle Farmers Market. There were other jobs too—bus driver, a couple of teachers, leather worker, custodian, fast-food restaurant worker (one little boy said that both of his parents worked for McDonald's), moving company worker, gas station attendant, tattoo artist, as well as one employee of the quintessential Delaware company, a business called Services Unlimited.

The children's parents had been drawn to the area because Delaware is the land of easy money. By that I mean not that wages are high but rather that the state is in the business of fueling the dreams of all those Americans who spend, rather than save, almost all that they earn today. In fact, late twentieth-century Christiana possessed a collection of mine shafts leading to gold, platinum or titanium—in the form of the plastic cards that you fish out of your wallet. That is because the country's largest banks base their credit card operations in Delaware. Several of the children I talked to told me that either their mother or father, or in some cases both parents, work at USA Fidelity, First USA, Citibank Delaware, Discover Card, or MBNA. Delaware—the Delaware economy—thrives at least in part because we are a society of debtors.

Near the spot where dockworkers once unloaded barrels of flour from boats on the Christina River, telemarketers now ply their e-trades and reach the far corners of the country in the process. One hundred thousand dollars in credit if you will just say "yes" over the phone and answer a few questions! It is true that if every family of four in the United States receives 150 offers of credit cards in a single year, then those who work the telephones and load the mailbags in Delaware certainly have their work waiting for them, now that a goodly proportion of sales take the form of electronic transactions.[4] Those people who toil in the financial services industry in the vicinity of Christiana express their occupational identity, not through making things or meeting with people, but through the zip codes, e-mail addresses, and toll-free phone numbers they use to do their jobs.

This is not to say that good old-fashioned shopping is a thing of the past in Christiana. Indeed, the new New Castle County reaches its apex on a site that the Wilsons, sister and two brothers, once called home. The place where my aunt and I used to get our eggs on Saturday morning is now called Delaware Metroform and includes the Christiana Hospital, Delaware Technical and Community College, a collection of restaurants and strip malls, and the crowning jewel: the Christiana Mall. Located about a mile from the Corner and right off I-95, with four flagship department stores, 150 smaller stores, a multiplex cinema, an expansive food court, and, as they say, ample free parking, Christiana is where New Jersey, Pennsylvania, Maryland and Delaware all meet 362 days a year, to shop, to eat, and to promenade.

Developers found the site attractive for a number of reasons. The land was cheap and the local county zoning commissioners compliant. The burgeoning housing developments in the immediate area, combined with the relative proximity of Wilmington and Philadelphia to the northeast and Baltimore to the southwest, assured large crowds of people year-round. Close by the mall are sprouting the so-called "boxes," superstores that sell everything from pet food to books and lawnmowers. Although Christiana has lost its character as a small town, it has retained its commercial function and its significance as a crossroads of real and symbolic importance within the contemporary regional economy.

These days the state of Delaware itself only rarely makes an impression upon the national consciousness. The biggest news stories of the 1990s (those that received inordinate national as well as local attention) were not Delaware stories at all, but rather events revealing of a more general fascination with the bizarre, the gruesome, the sensational. These included the 1996 murder of Anne Marie Fahey by Thomas Capano, a wealthy lawyer. His conviction three years later received more attention locally than the Clinton impeachment hearings. Local media also sensationalized the 1997 murder of the Peterson-Grossberg infant by its parents, both of whom had grown up in upper-middle class New Jersey suburbs and were now attending college (the mother at the University of Delaware, the father at Gettysburg College).

In certain key respects Delaware was a typical state in the year 2000. It ranked sixth in the nation in terms of per capita personal income ($27,782 in 1996), although here it should be noted that the average for New Castle County—$31,589—was considerably higher than that of either Kent or Sussex Counties (about $21,000 each). The state's relative prosperity, rendered in terms of averages, testified to the continued significance of high-paid chemical engineers and industry and banking executives. The black population of about 20 percent was evenly divided among all three counties, though Sussex County was unique by virtue of the relatively large increase in the Hispanic population through the decade of the 1990s, a growth of 250 percent from 1990 to 1996. More than sixty percent of the state's residents traced their ancestry to Western Europe (Ireland, Germany, and England), while twenty percent were African American and about 15 percent were descended from Poles and Italians. The state was average in terms of the size of its households (2.56 persons each), and average in terms of the educational attainment of its citizens (that is, higher than the Deep South but not as high as New England or some of the surrounding Mid-Atlantic states).

When I return home I find in Delaware, in stark relief, the larger historical processes, and especially the economic transformations, that have been the subject of my recent scholarship. Though unique by virtue of the prominence of its financial services industry, the state remains embedded in the Delaware Valley, a region characterized by manufacturing and oil refining. Consequently, the global economy now reaches deep into the collective livelihood of Delaware residents. For example, in 1999 the economic crisis in Asia had a direct impact upon production in Philadelphia-area factories. In Wilmington, Hercules Incorporated, one of the world's largest manufacturers of chemicals used in paper-making and other industrial processes, suffered from a slowdown in its earnings when the Asian demand for its products slacked and its pulp and paper wholesalers had to contend with swollen inventories.

Although the overall state labor force was increasing, employees in the military and agricultural sectors were declining both numerically and proportionately, the first group as a result of cutbacks at the Dover Air Force Base and the second group as a result of business consolidation and technological innovation in downstate agriculture. One exception within the latter category was Perdue Farms, Inc., a chicken processing firm that was tied with First USA Bank as the thirteenth largest employer in the state, with 2,300 wage earners. The case of the poultry industry in particular suggests the costs of growth and economic development. The phosphorous from chicken manure, together with chemical fertilizers and pesticides, forms a toxic farm runoff that has been blamed for breeding the fish-killer microbe *pfiesteria piscida* and polluting downstate rivers and creeks.

Over the last four decades or so, manufacturing has declined in the state, consistent with the national trend, though DuPont, Astra Zeneca, Chrysler and General Motors rank in the top twelve largest employers. The automakers have had to adapt to stay in business. In the 1990s, the GM plant in Boxwood, near Newport, retooled to produce only Chevrolet Malibus. Chrysler received a boost through a merger with Daimler of Germany. Still, the overall state economy is driven by the national banks, and the Delaware Court of Chancery stands as the emblematic state institution, for that is where the big boys of technology, industry, and finance meet to sort out their respective shares of the marketplace.

Within the space of a couple of days—say, the randomly chosen weekend of January 22, 1999—the business section of the Wilmington *News Journal* takes the form of a great social ledger of sorts. On one side are reports that during 1998 the state attained a decade-long high in job growth (12,700 new jobs, the bulk of them in the service sector) and that quarterly profits have soared for Chase Manhattan Corporation, Bank America, First USA Bank, J. Morgan and Bank One (all with credit card operations in the state). On the other side we find that Zeneca Group PLC, the third largest British-owned drug manufacturer, will be merging with Astra Pharmaceutical and possibly moving its operations (which currently employ 3,000 people in New Castle County) out of state, to Pennsylvania. In addition, a large food-processing plant, the Draper-King Cole cannery in

Milton (Sussex County), will be laying off all 300 of its production-line workers (though not its sales, marketing and administrative staff). In explaining the decision to sell off its 6,000-acre holdings in the state, one company official says that Draper-Cole wants to "concentrate on what we do well by getting rid of a whole lot of other distractions."[5] In this brave new economy (as in the old one), the livelihoods of ordinary men and women count as mere "distractions" for supervisors and shareholders. Progress for some people inevitably produces distress for others.

Today the Delaware Economic Development Office is happy to furnish printouts of state population statistics and economic indicators, but on a sheet called "Estimates of the Population of Delaware Places" the town of Christiana is nowhere to be found (though Hartly, population 113, and Slaughter Beach, population 124, are). Nevertheless, the name Christiana is ubiquitous throughout the county and the state—hospitals, malls, housing developments and banks use Christiana in their titles, though not all of them are located anywhere near the small town where I grew up.

Not too long ago someone who lives in Newark was talking about the community of Christiana, when he suddenly checked himself and said, "But of course there is no community any more. There is only the mall." In assessing the changes that have taken place in Christiana over the last four decades or so, we might consider the built environment first and the demographic profile second. In both respects, a child of the 1950s would hardly recognize the place.

Visually, the town's transformation has been striking. The fate of the Corner is emblematic. Baldwin's store is gone, razed to the ground. The firehouse has expanded, purchased a couple of ambulances, invested in state-of-the-art trucks, gobbled up several houses, and paved over a large area on one side of the Corner. (It has also retained a great deal of its vitality as a fraternal order: "Valentine Beef and Beer $30 couple" reads the sign in the parking lot.) In the spring of 2000, the interior of the Shannon Inn stood exposed for all the world to see. County officials ordered the owner of the building to tear down the brick facade, which was in danger of collapsing into West Main Street. Passersby could now admire the graceful wood moldings surrounding the fireplace in the main room of the first floor, where the town's merchants had once gathered to talk about grain shipments and Federalist politics.[6]

A development of modest townhouses ("Christiana Village") sits across the street from the Jones school. The former houses of my friends have met with varying fates—one is the site of a gas station, another has been obliterated by a cloverleaf leading on and off Route 95. Down the road on Route 7 a friend's farmhouse is still standing, but it now houses offices for a new apartment complex, Christiana Meadows. (The word Christiana precedes any number of subdivisions—in addition to Meadows, there are Acres, Court, Falls, Farms, Green. On the other hand, right outside town is the oddly named Norwegian Woods.) A Day's Inn Hotel occupies the spot where the Harvey farm once stood. Not far from that, a six-story office building, resplendent with mirrored windows, sits forlorn and empty, a "For Lease" sign its single adornment. Melinda Taylor's house has been converted to offices for an accounting firm, and my grandmother's house is a day care center called First Experiences.

My mother's house, now encircled by highways (one of them elevated), sits across from a Park and Ride lot. The pond is full of mud and silt, runoff from the traffic-choked roads that border it. The paths that I once explored are obliterated, overgrown with sumac and brambles. Located at the bridge that spans the once-mighty Christina is a sign, a picture of a dinner plate with a line drawn diagonally across it and the words "It is recommended that fish taken from these waters not be eaten." I guess not: There is a small sewage treatment plant near the bank of the river, and on certain days the stench pervades the air. The Christina, now a source of pollution and not commerce, has prompted a new kind of creek walking. Beginning in the early 1990s, the annual Christina River Watershed Cleanup sponsors an annual spring cleanup of the river's banks. In 1999 about a thousand volunteers, assigned to ten sites the length of the river, collected more than twenty tons of trash.[7] The creek walker in Ms. Lyle's class no doubt will have to double his efforts in the face of ever diminishing returns from his after-school ramblings.

If Christiana has much of an existence at all, it derives from the multiplicity of commercial enterprises that blanket what used to be called the Christiana-Salem school district. The town suffers from a bad case of big and small mall-sprawl. Between the Corner and the Jones Elementary School is a horseshoe-shaped collection of shops, Peddler's Village, which includes its own miniature version of a flagship store, Peddler's Liquors, and a variety of other establishments with high rates of turnover: Stop and Shop Software, Nationwide

Insurance, Milady Nails, Delaware Paralyzed Veterans, Diamond State Chiropractic, Physical Therapy and Spine Center, Wing Nuts, Arts of China, and Nationwide Insurance, among others. The beauty parlor that once found a home in Peddler's Village closed when, a few years ago, the husband of one of the hairdressers entered the premises and shot her dead. As far as I know, this was Christiana's first and only murder.

A little past the school sits University Plaza, a much larger strip mall with a Burlington Coat Factory and assorted furniture and shoe stores. The Acme grocery store draws customers from a wide area. In the parking lot one occasionally sees the cabs of huge tractor trailers; now separated from their loads, they serve as vehicles of choice for errand-runners. The Acme's shelves are stocked with three-pound cans of black-eyed beans, peanut butter, and spaghetti sauce, and the gigantic packaged meat section gives evidence of a community where many of the adults, and not just school children, pack a lunch every morning.

Bear, located along the convergence of Routes 13 and 40, now boasts dozens of new housing developments, including apartments like Brandywine Woods (according to an ad in *Delaware Today*, "A gated apartment community with all the features of a luxury resort!"), townhouses, and modest single-family homes. Bear has its own huge K-Mart and an impressive assortment of fast-food restaurants. For a while at least, by appealing to renters, downscale townhouse subdivisions (including one not far from the long-defunct Merry Land Roller Rink) were attracting low-income families from Philadelphia; their housing vouchers allowed them to escape the inner city and resettle in suburban New Castle County. However, this concentration of very poor people perpetuated the very ills that many of its residents were trying to leave behind—drugs, gangs, violence. The once inviolable boundaries between city and suburb blur and disappear. My mother's house, hit by a series of burglaries in the 1970s and 1980s, is now fortified with a sophisticated alarm system, so she must complete a series of complicated procedures necessary in order to secure the house before we run up to the Acme for a few minutes. I think of the days when everyone left their houses and car doors unlocked, and I feel very old. My mother, however, seems to have adjusted to this situation better than I.

Both Bear and Christiana illustrate another principle of New Castle County (and, by extension, modern-American) life—the fact that, combined with an explosion in the local population, super-stores of various kinds (Office Max, Borders, Home Depot) inevitably breed convoluted traffic patterns and super traffic snarls. With no signs of regional planners in evidence (though those more knowl-edgeable than I assure me they exist), New Castle County now con-sists of knots of highway intersections, where two or more four-lane highways cross each other and the car backups stretch for miles. Motorists thus enjoy extended opportunities to sit and reflect upon the excesses of commercial and residential development. I realize now that the territorial imperatives exhibited by the State Highway Department in the 1950s were but a dress rehearsal for the full-blown disaster that is northern Delaware today. Loose zoning regulations and the overweening power of the county government (to the detri-ment of the towns) have doomed small communities in the northern part of the state. No local institutions exist to counter the development-mad County Council.

Thus far this brief history of recent Christiana has stressed the twin themes of the physical destruction of the landscape on the one hand, and the ensuing problems, social no less than vehicular, on the other. The sign at the Christiana Bridge—the modern equivalent of a skull and crossbones—is its defining symbol. And yet this bald-faced tale of woe constitutes only a part of the story.

In fact, it would not be difficult to construct a alternative narrative of Christiana's recent history, and focus on the hope for the future that is on display in Ms. Lyle's fourth-grade classroom. If you were travelling west from Christiana to Ogletown today, and decided to stop off at the roller rink surrounded by several housing develop-ments that were built in the 1950s, you would step into a space where black and white kids of all ages mingle freely with each other. Out in the rink, the crowd moves counterclockwise, some skaters faltering, others dodging in and out among the slower ones at breakneck speed, moving to the pounding organ music under flashing strobe lights. Gliding cooly, gracefully, through it all are the older teenagers, the best skaters, paid employees who are supposed to make sure that no one plays tag or skates backwards under such crowded conditions. Once in a while in the middle of a disco hit, as if on cue, four or five of these older skaters, black and white, male and female, will hook up in a little train, and holding on to the waist of the person in front of them, speed around the rink, half-gliding, half-dancing intricate lit-tle dance steps, swaying back and forth, together. This performance excites no attention from the regulars, who go about their business of circling the rink. But for someone who grew up nearby many years ago, segregated, it is a magnificent sight—the skill of the skaters, the new biracialism in the place that was once called Christiana Bridge.

One doesn't have to look far to find other signs of just how much things have changed in New Castle County overall—in the Christiana mall, black men in their shiny United Automobile Workers or Teamsters jackets, escorting their families from J.C. Penney to Hickory Farms; on the pages of the *News Journal*, pictures of the African American weekly columnists, feature stories of black historic figures like Mary Ann Shadd Cary,[8] and pronouncements from the African American politicians who are active at every level of local, county, and state government today. The new elementary school located in the vicinity of the obscure hamlet of Salem is called the Thurgood Marshall School. At the Bob Evans restaurant in Christiana, black and white co-workers eat lunch together during the week.

Laments over transformations in the landscape ignore the fact that a great many families have made a new home for themselves in New Castle County. If both parents work at the new service jobs the region has to offer, they can afford to buy a modest tract house in a new development and probably take their kids to Disney World at least once every few years. Unemployment in the county is low, inflation is low, and the K-Marts and SuperMax super stores are jammed to overflowing.

The truth of Christiana's recent history probably lies somewhere between these two scenarios—one tragic, the other triumphant. Together, some of the newcomers help to create a multiplicity of new churches but in the process the older ones, like the Christiana Presbyterian Church, lose members as their congregations age. The county's spectacular job growth rests on a precarious foundation called the global economy. Consequently a deepening economic crisis in Asia or Latin America will have a direct impact upon manufacturing in the Delaware Valley and in the country as a whole, causing layoffs and forcing consumers to put the brakes on their credit card purchases whether they like it or not. The nonunionized jobs of telemarketer and key punch operator do not pay much, and so they mandate that both husbands and wives must work if the family is to own their own home and buy a new car every few years. The traffic jams can make the most innocent errand a time-consuming, maddening ordeal. Auto-exhaust pollution blankets the whole region.

Still, the stucco house on East Main Street in Christiana remains an oasis of sorts. Pulling into the garage at the back of the house on a winter night, you can see lights twinkling through the bare branches of the trees that ring the pond. A major thoroughfare runs past the house, and cars are lined up at the intersection just a few hundred yards beyond. But in the spring it will be possible to sit in the dining room and see a deer venture out of the woods, the spot where the dump used to be, or to watch a proud family of Canada geese, including newborn babies, waddle up from the pond in search of the corn scattered in the backyard for their benefit. In 1999 my mother was still hosting the Phelps family annual Fourth of July picnic. Her sisters (the two who were still living in the area) and their husbands, together with several of my cousins, their children and my cousins' grandchildren, all gathered on "the point" to play horseshoes and eat hamburgers and hot dogs. The crowd numbered as many as fifty people. But no matter how muggy the day, nobody was swimming in the pond any more because it was too dirty.

One night not too long ago, two old-oldtime Christiana residents sat in the Brown's Lane living room of one and talked about the changes they had witnessed over the last three-quarters of a century. Though the two women had grown up only a mile or so away from each other, they had always attended separate schools—one had gone to Christiana 111-C and then on into Howard High School in Wilmington, the other to Christiana 44 and then on to Newark High School. However, beginning in 1956, their daughters had attended the same school and had become friends. Their husbands, both deceased within the last few years, had worked their entire lives for the DuPont Company. Both women had sisters close by, practically next door. Their several children had scattered (one daughter lived with her family in Bear but the rest were in Massachusetts, Florida, and North Carolina). The two commiserated about the baleful effects of rapid population growth: the traffic, *the traffic!* They exchanged sighs over their aging and sadly static church congregations: the Presbyterian church was holding on with eighty members, but the United African Methodist Episcopal was down to only eighteen. The Brown's Lane community had changed perceptibly—now there were as many white folks living there as blacks—and the bad news was that a developer had already begun to bulldoze the parcel of land at the end of the street, the place where Maggie Rivers and her family had lived in the basement of their house always under construction.

The two women pondered the absurdity of it all—another strip mall in Christiana—and wondered what kinds of new stores the residents of the area could possibly need, what with Peddler's Village, University Plaza and Christiana mall all within a mile or so of each other. Where was the County Planning Commission in all of this?

Toward the end of their conversation that afternoon the two women turned to the subject of preserving the town's history. They both belonged to the Christiana Historical Society, a small group of elderly residents who held periodic meetings and managed to pay the $20 annual state licensing fee for the society each year. Early on they had set their sights high—to renovate the old Shannon Inn—but recently they had turned their attention to the abandoned structure that was once the pride of the state's African American community, 111-C, the school that Pierre S. DuPont had dedicated in 1920. A few years ago a fire had swept through it and now it was only a charred shell. Without more members, and without younger and more energetic members, the Historical Society would find it impossible to rebuild the school. The many newcomers now living in the area had little interest in the history of Christiana, their days consumed by work and family. On the other hand, the principal of the Jones Elementary School had recently announced that restoration of the burned building would be his pupils' "penny project" for the coming year. Here at least was a project that linked Christiana's past to its present and future.

Gradually, though, even history will disappear from Christiana. Ever since the canals and railroads passed the town by in the early nineteenth century, its residents lacked a distinctive identity shaped by either economic function or political vision. In the 1950s the town at least possessed the shape of a identifiable settlement, for the Corner and the four churches and the school and the firehouse provided it with a physical center. Now, with the encroachment of shopping malls and the proliferation of housing developments, it was possible for a passerby to travel through the town without even recognizing that it was there. The collection of ramshackle old buildings bespoke not days of past prosperity, but rather a neglected and no longer useful past, a past overwhelmed by gas stations and super stores.

The demise of the town represents a late twentieth-century Rorschach test of sorts. If Christiana once preserved a slice of Delaware's backward, racist past, then perhaps it is time to say good

riddance to it and move on. If, on the other hand, in its new incarnation it embodies a kind of hopefulness, then the expansive parking
lots and the infinite number of fast-food restaurants are to be hailed
as beacons that will continue to lead us toward a more prosperous
future, or at least to bigger and better end-of-the-year bargains at the
mall. But then again, perhaps either view would place more of an
historical burden on this little place than it can possibly bear.

I offer no elegy for the Christiana I knew as a child. Families form
and eventually their children leave home. That is the nature of com-
munities today as in the past, and that is the nature of the United
States, with its history of restless populations arriving from Riga and
Minsk like my in-laws' forebears, or relocating from New England to
Delaware like the Phelpses, or moving from the mid-Atlantic to New
England like my own family. Christiana is unique not because of the
series of dramas of economic change enacted on the banks of the
Christina, the cyclical ups and downs, but because the town has
managed to endure as a crossroads, accommodating disparate, suc-
cessive forms of commercial exchange over the last four centuries.
And I predict that, the best efforts of the annual Watershed Cleanup
notwithstanding, the river will continue to afford pleasures for those
skilled in the ways of the creek walkers.

Notes

CHAPTER 1: DELAWARE BUFFALO

1. Annette Woolard, "A Family of Firsts: The Reddings of Delaware," (Ph.D. diss., University of Delaware, 1994), 188.
2. Richard M. Keenan, *The Twentieth Air Force Album* (San Angelo, Texas: Newsfoto Books, 1982), 25. See also Robert E. Laird, *Maximum Effort: A First-Hand Account of a World War II Crew and Their Bomb Group*, n. p., n. d.

CHAPTER 2: CHRISTIANA BRIDGE

1. Amandus Johnson, *The Swedish Settlements on the Delaware*, vol. 1 (1638–1664) (New York: Burt Franklin, 1911), 187.
2. John Munroe, *History of Delaware* (Newark: University of Delaware Press, 1984), 15–16; Lorraine E. Williams, "Indians and Europeans in the Delaware Valley, 1620–1655," in Carol E. Hoffecker, *et al.*, eds., *New Sweden in America* (Newark: University of Delaware Press, 1995), 113–19.
3. Carol Hoffecker, *Delaware: A Bicentennial History* (New York: W. W. Norton, 1977), 7–13.
4. See for example Francine Prose, "Entering New Castle," *New York Times Sunday Magazine*, Part 2: *The Sophisticated Traveler*, Feb. 27, 2000, 62–70.
5. Ibid., 16–7.
6. C. A. Weslager, *Delaware's Forgotten River: The Story of the Christina* (Wilmington, DE: Hambleton Company, 1947) 16.
7. Ibid., 9.
8. Ibid, 8–9.
9. Harold Hancock, "The New Castle County Loyalists," *Delaware History* 4 (September 1951): 322, 327, 349–53.
10. Quoted in John Munroe, *Federalist Delaware, 1775–1815* (New Brunswick: Rutgers University Press, 1954), 251.
11. Francis A. Cooch, *Little Known History of Newark, Delaware and Its Environs* (Newark, DE: The Press of Kells, 1936), 7.
12. Harold B. Hancock, ed., "William Yates's Letter of 1837: Slavery, and Colored People in Delaware," *Delaware History* 14 (April 1971): 208.
13. In his classic book, *The Organization Man*, William H. Whyte cites the DuPont mid-level manager as the archetypical "organization man."

Chapter 3: Razzle-Dazzle

1. E-mail communication from Janetta Jackson, Feb. 14, 2000, in author's possession.

2. Ronald L. Lewis, ed., "Reverend T. G. Stewart and 'Mixed'Schools in Delaware, 1882," *Delaware History* 19 (Spring-Summer 1980): 57.

3. See Richard Kluger, *Simple Justice: The History of Brown v. Board of Education and Black America's Struggle for Equality* (New York: Knopf, 1976).

4. My senior thesis in college consisted of a brief history of this group. See "'Practical Christianity': The Delaware Association for the Moral Improvement and Education of the Colored People," *Delaware History* (1972).

5. Robert J. Taggart, "Christiana's Educational Heritage," study funded and published by the Delaware Humanities Forum (pamphlet), c. 1980.

6. Annette Woolard, "A Family of Firsts: The Reddings of Delaware," (Ph.D. diss. University of Delaware, 1994), 62.

7. Kluger, *Simple Justice*, 677.

8. Ed Kee, "The Brown Decision and Milford, Delaware, 1954–1964," *Delaware History* 27 (Fall-Winter 1997–1998): 205–44. The Bowles quotation is on 219.

9. Carol E. Hoffecker, *Delaware: A Bicentennial History* (New York: W. W. Norton, 1977), 83.

10. This quotation is taken from a typescript titled "Early History of Christiana Presbyterian Church (Taken from Two Talks Prepared and Delivered by Reverend Samuel L. Irvine, Minister)" (October 1934 and October 1937). Copy in author's possession. Other information related to the history of the church is contained in Betty J. Baird, "A Proud Heritage!" (1967), pamphlet, and two undated manuscripts, "Early Church Government 18th and 19th Century's [*sic*]" and "Christiana Pres. Church c. 1941–6," copies of which are in the author's possession.

11. Samuel L. Irvine, "Early History of Christiana Presbyterian Church," typescript in the author's possession.

12. Quoted in William H Williams, "Delaware and the Methodist Revolution," *Delaware History* 22 (Fall-Winter 1987): 273.

13. Irvine, "Early History of Christiana Presbyterian Church."

Chapter 4: Blood in the Salad

1. Sylvia Jones, "A Christiana Village Childhood," in "I Remember When: Between the World Wars, a Treasury of Reminiscences by Delaware Area Senior Citizens" (Newark: University of Delaware, 1980). My mother's prize-winning essay, from which this passage was excerpted, was included in this collection, which was sponsored by Cultural Affairs, Continuing Education, University of Delaware.

2. Richard Kluger, *Simple Justice: The History of Brown v. Board of Education and Black America's Struggle for Equality* (New York: Knopf, 1976), 429.

3. *Soldiers of Light and Love: Northern Teachers and Georgia Blacks, 1865 to 1873* (Chapel Hill: University of North Carolina Press, 1980).

4. *Labor of Love, Labor of Sorrow: Black Women, Work, and the Family from the Civil War to the Present* (New York: Basic Books, 1985).

5. *The Dispossessed: America's Underclasses from the Civil War to the Present* (New York: Basic Books, 1992).

6. Edmund Morgan, *American Slavery, American Freedom: The Ordeal of Colonial Virginia* (New York: W. W. Norton, 1975).

7. *American Work: Four Centuries of Black and White Labor* (New York: W. W. Norton, 1998).

8. *A Social History of the Laboring Classes from the Colonial Period to the Present* (London: Blackwell Publishers, 1999).

EPILOGUE: CREEK WALKERS AT THE MILLENNIAL CROSSROADS

1. Jeffrey A. Raffel, *The Politics of School Desegregation: The Metropolitan Remedy in Delaware* (Philadelphia: Temple University Press, 1980).

2. Ibid.

3. Data culled from materials provided by Delaware Economic Development Office, State Data Center, 99 Kings Highway, Dover DE 19903, including data collected by the United States Department of Commerce, Bureau of the Census, 1996–1998.

4. See for example Michael Rosenbaum, "A Credit Card for Every Occasion," *New York Times,* January 30, 1999, A27.

5. Articles in the Wilmington *News Journal,* Jan. 22, 1999, B1.

6. See Robin Brown, "Work Progresses on Shannon Inn," Wilmington *News Journal,* April 10, 2000, B3.

7. Edward L. Kenney, "Volunteer Crews Clean Up Along the Christina River," *Sunday News Journal,* April 16, 2000, B1.

10. Gary Soulsman, "Overlooked Warrior," *News Journal* July 10, 1998, Section D, 1.

Index